A WITCH ALONE

A WITCH ALONE

Thirteen moons to master natural magic

Marian Green

Thorsons
An Imprint of HarperCollinsPublishers

Thorsons
An Imprint of HarperCollins*Publishers*
77–85 Fulham Palace Road
Hammersmith, London W6 8JB

Published by The Aquarian Press 1991
Published by Thorsons 1995
18 20 19

A catalogue record for this book
is available from the British Library

ISBN 1 85538 112 5

Typeset by Burns & Smith Limited

Printed and bound in Great Britain by
Creative Print and Design (Wales), Ebbw Vale

CONTENTS

Dedication

To Tony
Long term friend and
companion on the
Inner Ways

Song of the All-Mother

I am the Mother Earth, and you're a Child to me,
Discover who you are and seek divinity.
Rocks and stones and clay and peat – all strata are a part of me,
Jewels and crystals, gems and gold are hidden in the heart of
   me.
Herbs and flowers, trees and shrubs, these are growing green
   on me,
Mosses, fungi, lichens, vines, all of these are seen on me.
Horses, cattle, pigs and deer, bears and lions roam on me,
Snakes and spiders, rats and slugs, all creatures have their
   home on me.
Bubbling brooks and silent springs, living rivers flow on me,
Pools and puddles, lakes and seas, salty oceans grow on me.
Tiny tiddlers, mightly whales, sacred salmon leap for me,
Sharks and squid and crabs and krill fill the waters deep for
   me.
Wrens and larks and crows and terns fill my skies with
   darting flight,
Hawks and eagles, bats and owls catch their prey by day and
   night.
Creeping worm and flying fox, teeming ants fulfil their lives,
In tune with me, in Nature's way, as honey bees enrich my
   hives.
Only humans rob their kin, despoil the land, pollute the seas,
Kill for fun, destroy the woods, float poisoned vapours on the
   breeze.
I shall live, for I can heal, even if you humans die,
But you can learn, as Children should, to grow in peace
   beneath the sky.

Lord of the Wildwood

A silence lies on the Wildwood,
The light of the stars grows dim,
The wind has died in the branches,
But a shadow moves. It is Him!
He is the stag in the moonlight,
The stallion alone on the hill,
The bull that paws at the tussocks,
The salmon that leaps in the rill.
Each is a part of the Hunter,
The Godhead that lives in the Dark,
Lord of the Wild and the Hidden,
At midnight, the small breathing spark.
His is the glory of sunrise,
The greenness that rises in spring,
His is the force of the tempest,
The strength in the wild eagle's wing.
His is the voice of the pan-pipes,
The power that governs the land,
But *She* is his wife and his Mother,
And he dwells in the palm of her hand.

The Paradoxical Goddess

Lady of the threefold shifting light,
Whose form is Earth, by day and night,
And yet about you flows eternal ocean,
Goddess so still, yet in perpetual motion.
Moon, sister-self and triple aspect of the Triple One,
Maiden, God creator, wise and ancient Crone.
Thou who art Earth, and Moon, and Sea,
Mother of All, thou madest me.
From your dark bones, from green and flesh,
From crystal waters and the quiet wind's breath,
These came from you, and now are me,
Eternal spirit clothed in frailty.
Yet beyond these there endless dwells
A light that from some star-seed fell.
Goddess of Life and Love and Paradox,
Keeper of the keys to all the locks,
Of Mysteries, of Earth and Sky,
Pray answer me. Who am I?

INTRODUCTION

I am brother to dragons and companion to owls . . .
Old Testament; Job 29:30

Many people are drawn, these days, to the idea of witchcraft.
Some seek religious freedom, some wish for magical powers,
some wish to reawaken the ancient links with our Mother
Earth, or seek healing of both body and spirit.

Some wish to be part of covens, to share ceremonies and
regular meetings with like-minded folk in the comfort of their
own homes. Others, however, have heard wilder music,
playing to an older beat, and wish to reunite with Mother
Nature, alone, out of doors, under the light of the stars and
changing moonlight, in a simpler way. It is for those people I
am writing this book. Those who seek covens have been well
served by recent publications and they will find the contacts
they require if they look diligently, but others who do not wish
to join with a group, or cannot because of their work or family
commitments, those who wish to master the ancient arts of
magic, the personal pagan faith, the various ancient crafts *alone*,
may need this guidance.

The solo occult path is a traditional one, following in the
footsteps of the oracle, the hermit, the shaman or Druid priest.
Even those who are able to share the festivals and healing rites
with others may wish to develop their personal spiritual
dimensions, gaining self-confidence and power as an individual
witch as well as a member of a coven. But the solo path in any
study is hard, and that which leads through the hidden worlds
of witchcraft perhaps even more so, because it is dealing with
intangible things, with 'inner worlds', with gods and goddesses,
and ancient myths and magic. Much of the work involves

dealing with symbols, with mysterious forces, and seeing with illuminated vision things invisible to the ordinary, waking eye. Beginners will have to get used to dealing with the past, and the future, or aligning themselves with a new pattern of celebrations and milestones in the turning year, with the phases of the moon and with their own inner tides. They will have to make contact with the gods and goddesses, but they will find that the Mighty Ones are gentle, treating those nervously taking their first tentative steps into the world of magic as delicate chicks or small children. It does not mean that they are always so mild, and the student will soon discover their fiercer faces can be shown to protect or ward off interference. The kindliest goddess can still scold her children if their demands are excessive.

The purpose of this book is to show those who seek an alternative way that they may worship the pagan deities on their own, that they may master the ancient arts and magical crafts, just as their ancestors may have done. We may be living in a 'global village', but it still has a need for its traditional servants, the modern equivalent of a tinker, tailor, butcher, baker and candlestick-maker. It will need a healer who can see beyond the confines of the body and the limitations of a single symptom. It will need someone to set out the rituals which mark the times and tides; it will need a clairvoyant to plan for the future, and one with vision, who can look back into the far past and recover from that source lost wisdom for the waiting world.

Only the witch-finders said, 'Thou canst not be a witch alone!' History shows that each community had its own wise woman, calling her midwife, prophet, herbalist or comforter. Some of these were accused of crimes, tried and executed. Most were innocent, for those with the true knowledge kept their secrets, knew the future and took care to be hidden if the inquisitors came along. Their knowledge has not been lost; it has been hidden, forgotten and overlooked among many fragments of country life.

Among the half-remembered customs, traditional tales, old songs, folk plays and dances are the keys to a great store of wisdom, unwritten lore and magical arts. To reopen that storehouse may be a simple matter for those with common sense, and an enquiring mind. Those who care for the world, who honour Nature and wish for healing and harmony, those are the people who may rediscover the Earth Mother and inherit her bounty in this modern world.

All traditional crafts and magical skills have to be learned alone, for they are the technologies of the trained mind, the awakened heart, the keen eye, able to see other worlds than this. The religion of the newborn pagan has to come from the heart too, for there is no book, no dogma, no appointed priesthood to interpret scriptures written on the wind. The Old Ones are immanent; they are kindly although they have been miscalled, ignored, forgotten and maligned by followers of a newer faith. They do hear our prayers, give inspiration, offer consolation and guidance, and bless us with wholeness, if we ask them patiently and sincerely. We have to seek them out in their old territory, the woods and downs, the high hills and the river valleys, on mountain peaks and in secret caves. Their voices may be heard on the wind, in the cries of birds, and the laughter of falling water. To know them is an individual quest for they have no man-made dwellings, they are too great to be contained in four walls. They are sunlight and moonshine, starlight and the inner light that shines from the newly kindled fire within each one who walks in their ways. Their worship is joy and rejoicing and their rituals are freedom of the spirit, dancing in harmony with Nature, life-long to a peaceful end. Their benediction is in quiet rain which will bring cleansing, and in starlight, which will bring hope, and in the light of the moon which will offer inner vision to those who wish to see.

What I am writing is not 'gospel', it is not holy writ carved on tablets of stone, but a treasure trove of ideas, gleaned from the fields of life over many years. Working with various pagan and witch teachers, with healers and folk-herbalists, with ordinary country folk long steeped in traditional lore, I have gathered all sorts of experiences over the last thirty or so years. From these I have tried to set out a pattern of training, of practical exercises, of mental and psychic arts which can help any individual find a way to the doors of 'Witchdom', and a path to the feet of the Goddess, from whom, ultimately, all knowledge, magic and power flows.

This is not an easy path to follow, nor is it for all. Those who set out upon the hidden ways need to desire that secret knowledge, long for it in their hearts, yearn for it in their souls, and be willing, in turn, to offer continuing personal dedication, commitment and love. It is not a religion anyone should be forced to follow by outsiders, but an internal upwelling of feeling of belonging to the Earth Mother and her consort, the

Lord of the Wild. Worship and prayer should be natural experiences, becoming a regular part of all witches' daily life, as each one actually comes to know the forms of the Great Ones, their wisdom and power to change our lives. Like all human relationships, there has to be a coming together, a recognition of kinship, and an on-going desire to strengthen and renew that unity. Without these inner urges acts of ritual, of magic and of seasonal celebration are sham, and worthless in the eyes of the Eternal.

If you feel drawn to the old ways, to the rediscovery of abilities you have overlooked in this modern world, to a religious experience which offers direct and personal revelation to aspects of deities you will come to know, then perhaps the lessons and ideas set forth in this book will be helpful. It is only a guide book, a map of a possible journey, a description of what someone else has seen and felt. You will have to make the journey for yourself, being aware of your own circumstances, commitments to job and family, allocation of time and other resources. None of the paths of magic leads away from the world, setting you free from life's troubles at a stroke; they lead you deeper in. They show you with unveiled eyes the reality of situations, relationships, and the need to come to grips with your own problems and solve them. The inner worlds are not an escape, but a harsh training school where the will is forged, the soul laid bare to the light of Truth, and any weaknesses shown clearly by the wisdom of the ages.

There will be many strange ideas to examine, many ancient arts to rediscover, much lore and folk tale, myth and symbol to be assimilated before it can be used. Magic offers many paradoxes, and you will undergo 'culture shocks' as your growing powers, abilities and sensitivity develop.

At the end of each chapter you will find a list of books to read, but these are by no means the only books worth looking at. Seek out others by the same authors or on the same subjects. It is possible that brand new titles which will help with your build-up of knowledge are being published now, so be willing to write to the various publishers and request their most up-to-date catalogues, or go on their mailing lists. Use your public library, requesting them to order some of the rarer or older books which may now be out of print. Don't scorn book learning, but don't imagine either that it holds all the wisdom you need.

You will also find, both in each chapter and at the end, some practical exercises for you to try. This is a matter for serious commitment, not just a skimmed read-through. Magic is at its most demanding and dangerous when it is dabbled with, so either try hard to work through the series of exercises in order, or ignore them altogether until you are ready. Many of them, like the mental exercises of Meditation in its various forms, Creative Visualization or Inner Journeying, Concentration, and understanding Symbols, are studies which will continue throughout your magical career, if you become willing to do the on-going work. Although these are taught here within an occult framework, you will discover that they are equally valuable in the everyday world. If you can visualise it will aid your memory, if you can meditate you will be able to find calm in frantic moments, if you can concentrate you can solve all problems.

Ideally you should set aside a regular half-an-hour every day to study, read or try out the various old arts. Some of those periods ought to be out of doors, if only in a garden or park, so that you can learn about Mother Nature, sense her moods and changes. Some exercises can be shared with friends, some really do need a companion, and others are best tried alone. Do your best, and the gods will bless you.

1.

A NEW MOON AND A NEW DREAM

What Traditional Witchcraft is really about on its practical side is the hidden powers of the human mind. These can be aided by traditional knowledge of techniques which will bring them out and develop them; but basically the powers of witchcraft, shamanism, magic or whatever one likes to call it are latent in everyone. This is one of the first things I was taught by Gerald Gardner also, so it is something about which there is a general agreement as a basic teaching.

Doreen Valiente: *The Rebirth of Witchcraft*

As we approach the end of the century, many people are looking for new directions, in life, in philosophy and in religion. Some have set out on strange paths, beckoned on by the ideas and practices of foreign cults. Others have looked for a more homely, familiar tradition to follow, but this latter path is overgrown and lost in the modern world. Yet the longing remains. Somewhere there is a form of religious expression which appeals to the heart, is without dogma, brings the seeker close to the deities, from which spiritual comfort, healing and guidance may be received at first hand. Since the 1950s such a faith has been re-emerging under the title of 'Witchcraft'. Witchcraft is not just a pagan religion, however, for it has at least two other interesting components. One is magic and the other encompasses a wide array of traditional crafts, from using herbs in healing to making talismans and charms.

Witchcraft, as a religious impulse, has never gone out to recruit or convert those of other faiths, nor does being a witch prevent you following an orthodox belief as well. Today there are Catholic witches, Quaker and Church of England witches, as well as Hindu, Jewish and Buddhist witches. The paganism of modern witchcraft is an expansive philosophy which holds all

aspects of life as sacred. Its mythology includes many forms of
gods and goddesses, both Classical pagan, like the pantheons of
ancient Egypt, Greece or the Celtic and Norse lands of the
North, as well as the magically born, annually dying and
sacrificed hero gods, which can include Attis or Jesus. It is
necessary to study all scriptures and holy books, and
mythologies too, to reassess their teachings and values for the
current world.

It is often thought that witchcraft involves the worship of a
character which the Christians call 'Satan', but this is *not true.*
The Satanists are not pagan witches but derive from
Christianity, perverting the usual understanding of Good and
Evil of that religion. Witches, on the whole, do not have any
kind of evil deity. They worship Mother Nature, the Great
Goddess who also rules over the triple phases of the Moon, and
all the Waters, be they springs, rivers or oceans. Her consort,
divine Son and Champion is the Lord of wild and tame
creatures; he is the Hunter, the Corn King, the dying and
reincarnating Sun God, bearing the antlers of the stag or the
sun's rays upon his brow. Each of these deities rules over
patterns of change, the natural rebirth of the Earth's green
bounty in spring, its summer burgeoning, autumnal decay and
winter rest. The Goddess *is* the Earth beneath our feet, our
home and the substance from which our physical bodies are
created. She is the water that refreshes and cleanses us, and the
moonlight which, with its ever-fluctuating light, enriches our
dreams, and if we are wise, awakens our magical powers of
psychic vision. The Sun God lights up our world, giving it life,
warmth and vital energy. Ultimately, it is from the Sun's power
that we receive our food for all green things are fuelled by solar
reaction, and where there is no light there is no life as we know
it.

In witchcraft there is no sense of 'having to believe' in an
Earth Goddess and a Sun God, but each one who comes freely
and of their own will to the Old Religion will come to *know*,
through personal revelation and religious experience, that
mighty powers can be encountered and prayed to, from whom
guidance, strength and healing can be genuinely received. The
seasonal festivals which mark the passing year enact the lives of
the Goddess and her Son/Consort, bringing their energies into
the sacred circle so that they may be communed with by all who
seek them. There is no dogma, just a body of myths and legends

handed down by country folk, the original *paganus*, in song and
rhyme, in dance and mime, in tale and half-remembered
calendar custom or traditional fair.

In earlier times, when almost everyone worked on the land or
at crafts and skills connected with natural produce, a sequence
of seasonal events punctuated the turning year with feasts and
festivals, gatherings and partings. In each village there would
be a number of families pursuing inherited crafts: the
blacksmith, the baker, the cobbler and, probably, the wise
one/herbalist/witch. Just as the blacksmith would teach the
magics of his skill with metals to his sons, so would the
healer/witch teach her children, so that the old knowledge
would be passed down, within the family, to both men and
women. The Cunning Men had their own Mysteries, trade
secrets if you like, as did the women, which would help them
discover lost cattle, cure sickness in mankind, beast or the land
itself, oversee the loves and hates of their community, offering
wise advice or charms and potions, as the client requested.
They would be the keepers of the community's songs which
spoke, since Celtic times, of every individual's lineage, his
grandsires and traditional crafts. They would know the herbs
that aided childbearing, or kept pregnancy from befalling. They
knew the plants which would bring peaceful sleep, or death, or
dreams of wild frenzy. They would watch the heavens, noting,
in their own unwritten code, the births of children, deaths of the
old, meetings and partings of lovers and their fingers were
always on the pulse of village life, their dark eyes at the
knotholes of the shutters, watching their narrow world go by.
Because they knew what was in the hearts of those who came
seeking love potions, or vengeance or luck, they could barter or
predict or manipulate the outcomes of any activities within their
magically delineated patch. They held the secrets of life and
death, and were feared or respected for their craft, their skills
and their magics.

And these old unwritten wisdoms live on, hidden in the
secluded and veiled world of 'Witchdom'. They are seldom
found in books, for most of the old arts are trivial, the spells
simple, the crafts are intuitive rather than learned in an
academic way. They are seldom found in covens, either, for
these modern groups of witches are directed by a High Priestess
and a High Priest, in regular rituals often held, perforce, inside
a house rather than out in the moonlight, where Mother Nature

holds all in her thrall. The covens offer friendship and shared worship, regular activities and initiation for those who seek that path. But it isn't the only way. Many excellent books have been written for coven witches, spelling out their ceremonies, degrees, philosophies and mythology, but this offers only one side of the coin.

Social history is very quiet about the lives, beliefs and activities of the common folk. Historians have looked at kings and bishops, leaders in battle or cloistered monks, recording their view of history on vellum. No one bothered with the peasants, nor the secretive crafts folk, plying their individual trades to serve their own community. No one travelled very far from the place they were born, unless service to the lord of the manor entailed their enforced attendance on a battle, uprising or work on his lands held at a distance. The few freemen, the journeymen carpenters, masons and clerics who did travel often huge distances to ply their specialist trades, were a fairly rare bunch, and they kept their own secrets closely. Many, however, protected and preserved the Old Religion wherever they went. Look in any old church and there you will probably find the Green God of Nature in the rafters as a Green Man, or the Goddess in her guise of deer or hare or rose of the world. These ancient pagan images have spent fifteen hundred years gazing down on followers of a newer faith below, yet they have not lost their magic.

Certain places in the wild have always held the aura of power: the summits of high and lonely hills, sacred springs within the hidden grove, deep caves, and the ancient, stone-encircled dancing grounds, recognised as holy by our long-lost ancestors, marked on their mind-maps which we, with awakened inner vision, may read anew. These are the protected places, the boundaries between earth and water, air and earth, this world and that of Witchdom, hidden only by a veil of dream. Go there alone, in the spirit of adventure and seek out the atmosphere, if nothing else. Feel the energy of any such place, quietly, inside your head. Ask that the Guardian Deity of the sacred area come to you and sit for a few minutes in silence, relaxed, with your eyes closed. Listen with sharp ears for the tread of the Goddess's feet on the land of that other world, feel the brush of her silken veil, the warmth of her breath, like the touch of the breeze upon your cheek. Sense the arrival of the Lord of Wild Animals, the heavy tread of a stag or bull, the rasp of hairy hide upon a tree's rough bark. These will not harm you, but welcome you upon the threshold of their realm. They will bless you and show you that there are other paths of faith, older gods, more immanent ones. They will not coerce or threaten, nor condemn the other ways we humans walk in our individual quests for religious understanding and a philosophy of life.

If you have a dream, to walk unfettered in the search for your true self, to find a way of living in harmony with the Earth and all Nature, to strive for balance between your own needs and those of the whole planet and the others who share it with you, perhaps one such direction may be found here. It is not for everyone. It is not something to be taken up as a momentary whim, or as a hobby or time-filler until something more exciting comes along. It is a hard journey, first within to the deepest and darkest recesses of your own heart, where all your failures, cruelties, selfishness and hurt lie uncovered, like some hidden dragon's hoard. This is the treasure of experience, through which you must pick your way, seeking the precious jewels, the holy relics, the forgotten or abandoned parts of you, the childhood ambitions, abilities and skills which every witch would value. Did you used to be able to fly in your dreams? Your wings are here. Could you judge character and motives, even when you were too young to have the words to tell this truth? Those words and insights are also here. Here are the desires to heal, to do good, to see fairies face to face, to ride the unicorn or shining serpent, to meet with the heroes or kings and queens of ancient myth. Here is your own Holy Grail.

The object of this book is not to spell out for you some ancient formula which will magically make you a 'witch', but to show you the paths along which you may walk in order to discover for yourself some of the many arts, crafts and religious aspects which the followers of the Old Religion used to have. Only the touch of the Goddess or the God can awaken your witchly ancestry within you, and that you will need to seek, when you are ready. In order to succeed you may need to change some of your ideas, and cast a few long-held theories out of the window. You will need to consider your responsibilities as one who works with power. You will need to see what ordinary commitments you may have to give up in order to devote time, energy or some other personal resource to your new-found interest. Nothing is gained for nothing. You will have to pay for your knowledge with dedicated and long-term effort, with patience and with small sacrifices of things you care about.

This book is intended to be a loose course of instruction, with areas of work to be tackled month by month. Turning to the end and trying out the suggestions there will not instantly make you a witch; it will just show your youth in spiritual matters which, like all other arts and skills, have to be learned step by basic step. Read the whole book through, see if it awakens old knowledge within you, or shows you, through those sudden flashes of insight, that you have simply forgotten much of the wisdom you had in other lives, or that dwells within your family's genetic legacy to you.

Because our country-dwelling ancestors had no truck with calendars or digital watches, this series of lessons is set in moon-long chunks, to be worked on from the day after each new moon, through the waxing phase to full moon, and through the waning until the day of the dark of the moon. Because we are literate and need to remind ourselves with written notes or computer entries, one of the first things you will need, when you are ready to seriously follow the instructions here, is a new diary or large-format book. It will become your personal log of progress or you could call it a 'Book of Illuminations'. To begin with you will need to know when there will be a new moon. It is far better to stick your head out of a window as it gets dark and look out for the moon, so she may show you her current phase. Remember, in the Northern hemisphere, the moon is a ☽ crescent as she waxes, and a ☾ shape as she wanes, and from one new moon to the next is 29 and a bit days. For convenience, this is usually taken as four weeks of seven days.

Before we used the Roman names of the months, country folk measured time passing by nights and moons. Around the country some fragments of this old lore endure, like calling the full moon of September the Harvest Moon, October the Hunter's Moon and so on. We still use the expression 'a fortnight', meaning fourteen nights, not days! Each lunar period was given over to some specific agricultural activity, weather permitting. There were times for sowing seed, for haymaking, cutting the corn, weeding, gathering fruits of orchard and woodland, for worrying about poor harvests and for rejoicing after rich ones. When there were no convenient shops to supply the bread and little money to buy food, the relationship with the Earth Mother was felt very closely. These days we seldom suffer such hunger, or concern for the coming of spring. The stresses of modern occupations cannot be compared with the fear of starvation, the desperation when the weather prevented the sowing of seed or reaping of harvests, or when the winter woodpile was depleted or the last peats burned, long before the snows had melted from the cottage roofs.

Begin to look around you and see in what ways the moon has affected your life, your home or even your job. Get out after dark and try to see the phase of the moon in the sky. Is the moon visible from your bedroom window, and does her light shine upon your face. What do you know about her phases? Is she the same the whole world over? What about astronauts landing on her surface, she who is a Goddess and bringer of psychic visions?

Do you think you might like to become a pagan, or develop the powers of a 'witch'? What will your family or workmates think? Will you meet with fear or derision from them? Who should you tell about your new interest? Who do you know who might be able to help you or share your experiments? Are there already any witches in your circle of friends and acquaintances? Would any of them have anything to say, or help to offer? Do you really wish to belong to a coven, to undergo initiation and become part of a fairly secret society? Or are you content in your own company, happy to wander around in natural surroundings, enjoying sunlight and the life of trees and herbs, of birds and wild creatures? Do you crave company, someone to pour out your troubles to, or give you encouragement in any of your wilder schemes? All these questions are important, because if you really do set out to become a 'witch' or follower of the Old Ways, some parts of your studies will set you apart.

You will probably lose a few friends, not because they come to fear you but simply because you no longer have the time and energy to devote to some shared activities. Some of your friends might scoff at your pagan ambitions, or make fun of your intentions in front of others, if they get to hear about your interest in witchcraft. Others might try to cause trouble in your job, or stir up bad feeling, through a lack of understanding of modern pagan ideas. You might encounter Fundamentalists of one sort or another, or those out to save your soul from some invented harm, and you will be well advised to consider what responses you might give to such people, if they turn up on your doorstep. Suggesting that you could turn them into a bat might seem to be a good idea at the time but such threats, even made in fun, can be taken too seriously by religious fanatics in whose faith there is little fun, light or laughter.

Among those of the Craft, however, you should find great joy, a real sense of fun and a lightness of spirit which can prove cheering when you feel lonely or despondent, because your meditations are barren, and the moon of your intuition is dark. Even if you are studying alone, you ought to be able to laugh at yourself. Think back to how you would see yourself as a witch, with the regulation pointed hat, the broomstick, cauldron and black cat. Do you imagine it would be amusing, huddled around a cauldron over the smoky fire, conjuring spirits to visible appearance, or brewing potions of bits of frog and noxious herbs in the company of cackling sisters of the art? Again, history has a little by way of explanation about the archetypal picture of the old witch, warts and all. When the first books with woodcut illustrations were printed in the 15th century, an old dame, accused of witchcraft, was depicted. She was dressed at the then height of fashion, in a long dark skirt, shawl and lacy cap topped by a tall hat with a round brim, a costume typical of Welsh ladies to this day, if you look at holiday postcards from that principality. Unfortunately, the image persisted, long after the fashions changed. The old lady, with her walking stick, trendy attire and her pet cat, became everyone's idea of how the witch is supposed to look. Pity that picture is now about six hundred years out of date!

In the Middle Ages, keeping an animal as a pet, whether it was a cat to keep down mice or a dog to hunt the odd rabbit for the pot or even a toad or lizard, was thought to be very strange, and it is on the evidence of such a relationship that some poor old souls were accused, and even sometimes hanged, for their supposed involvement in witchcraft. Today some witches are vegetarians or even vegans, neither eating nor wearing animal products or having them in their homes. Many belong to animal protection or rescue services. Again, the suggestion that witches, then or now, killed animals or used their blood in spells is totally wrong. They would probably have eaten meat, when they could get it, for in the winter especially the country folk had a very poor diet compared to our modern, vitamin-enriched, prepackaged and out-of-season fare. However, the symbolic objects associated with the archetypal witch figure still have a relevance in today's Craft. Some covens have cauldrons,

broomsticks, even cats, because members of the Old Religion
have always been practical and kindly people. Objects which
have both a practical and a magical use have always been
sought by witches. Some of these are natural charms, fossils in
the shape of a leaf or an arrow-head collected from the fields or
river banks to act as protective amulets. Pebbles with an eye
shape turn up all over the world as charms against being
'overlooked' by someone with an evil eye. Perhaps a similar
charm ought to be discovered to attach to computers to prevent
hackers and ward off computer 'viruses'. Who knows what new
arts the New Age witch might need to develop!

The old cauldron was the ordinary cooking pot, yet it could
also be used to brew up herbal or magical potions, or the
simmering water in the dark iron pot would make an excellent
scrying mirror for seeing into the future. The broomstick,
whose homely task was to sweep the floor, became a magical
wand, and a swept area in the earth or rushes of a simple
cottage floor became the magical circle wherein the witch could
call up her powers to see at a distance, to seek answers to
questions, to raise the energy for healing or blessing a charm. If
you take up these old arts you will need to gather a few basic
tools around you. This is not the excuse to take your cheque
book to the nearest occult emporium and lay out large sums of
money for esoteric artefacts, equipment, robes, incenses, knives
and what-not. If you really want to master the Crafts of the
Wise you will do far better to look in your garden shed, in the
kitchen drawer, or in the attic for forgotten treasures which
your new-found arts will require.

Your first acts of magic, if you are one of the rare folk who
actually do want to align themselves with the traditional arts
and reawaken the creative powers of the Old Religion within
themselves, will be to get out of doors as much as you can. At
first it might seem strange, walking along familiar streets
among houses and shops, perhaps, with ancient or modern
buildings, or perhaps in the countryside. (On average about
85% of people interested in witchcraft in Britain today live in
towns or cities or other urban areas!) The difference is that you
will actually be opening your eyes and looking. Look at the
buildings, what are they made of? Look at the people, where
did they originate? Look at the trees, the plants in gardens or
parks, are they common to the land or new fancy species
introduced recently? Look at the roads and lanes, are they

straight or curving, following a buried stream perhaps, or some
other ancient boundary? Where is your nearest flowing water,
be it stream, river or even the sea coast? What do you know
about the tides and their relationship to the moon? Become
curious about everything, for that was certainly one of the assets
of every traditional witch. Seek to know about your
community, its needs, its desires, its good and bad points, and
above all, seek out your local magical spots.

There is no obvious way of locating the most sacred place in
your area, and as you are different from me, there is no way of
explaining what it might feel like to you. Perhaps you will feel a
tingle on the skin, a feeling of heat or cold, or sense the hairs
standing up on the back of your neck. Places to go and
examine, even in your untrained and unmagical state, should
be any kind of spring of water, the oldest church and its
churchyard, particularly ancient trees, historic buildings, ruins
or, of course, any local standing stones, circles, tumuli, barrow
mounds, henges, green ways, hill forts, hill figures, Roman
roads or even older causeways. If nothing else is suitable in your
home area, go to the top of the highest hill and start by watching
the sunset or the sunrise. Take a picnic, take grandma and the
kids, go and visit, in a relaxed and watchful mood, any such
place with ancient associations. Note down the phase of the
moon when you make your journey. Sit quietly and ponder,
muse or daydream, asking silently in your heart that you might
understand a little of the magic or sacredness of the place.
Gentle, new thoughts will drift through your head. Ideas will
seem to spring from nowhere. Be silent, still and patient. Feel
the earth beneath you, the sky above, and the eternal balance in
which they stand. Feel the ages rolling back so that the people of
the past, with their forgotten wisdom, may speak to you inside
your mind, or drift their shadows across your distracted eyes.
Be at peace, seek the calmness and enduring qualities of a big,
healthy tree, ask for the voice or energy of a bubbling brook or
the surging sea. Request the freedom of spirit to soar with the
gulls or skylarks, and see what happens. What ever you do, try
to understand the old ways, the simplicity and immediacy of
events in your ancestors' lives. Rediscover the skills they might
have had, the crafts they practised, the way they lived in
reasonable harmony with the earth, taking only what they
needed and harming her as little as possible.

These may seem like very small steps to take, but you will be surprised at how much you can discover by peeping over a few walls, examining the shape of your home town, looking out for the sorts of natural things which might well have been sacred to our ancestors. There is a simple logic to the things they considered holy, if you think about it. The sun raised and ripened the crops on which all life depended; the springs of fresh water offered to quench the thirst of man and beast, in summer droughts and winter snows. There is a life force in spring water very different from that in processed tap water, as is obvious from the increasing popularity of bottled spa and mineral waters. Our ancestors named this life force, found in healing springs and herbs, 'virtue' and valued its effects.

We are a literate people and fill our memories with telephone numbers, 'trivial' facts and figures, which may be useful on quiz programmes but are not a lot of help when it comes to the application of magical arts. So it is necessary to begin to build up new memories, data banks and bits of knowledge to apply to our new-found witchly crafts. Obviously, this is not going to be suddenly regained by sitting at the feet of our arcane grandparents, nor can we conjure back the simpler ages when all knowledge was absorbed, day by day, at our mother's knee, so we have to turn to books. Of course, there are lots with the word 'witchcraft' in the title, but not all contain useful material for the solo student, or one who wants to walk unhampered in the old ways. Do look out for the books of Doreen Valiente, for she was one of the people most closely involved in the rebirth of 'coven witchcraft', being one of Gerald Gardner's High Priestesses, and it is her poetry which gave voice to much of the pagan ritual used in groups all over the world. She learned much of her own lore from the Sussex folk and wove threads of that traditional wisdom into some of the more public of her writings. Gerald Gardner, in his novel *High Magic's Aid*, and other books *The Meaning of Witchcraft* and *Witchcraft Today*, first brought together enough ideas to set in train the forms of witchcraft which are used by many covens worldwide today. The various works of Stewart and Janet Farrar trace the varieties of coven craft spreading from the ideas of Alex Sanders, who mixed some of the arts of High Magic ritual into the fragments of craft knowledge he had accrued over many years. Read all such books with these questions ever in your mind, 'Can I imagine the simple, ordinary country folk doing this, using this instrument, or even being rich enough to possess a sword, for example? Would they gather in this way, have a structure of priests and priestesses, a regular calendar of feasts fixed by the days of the month, and not by Nature and her cyclic harvests?'

Whatever you read, try not to restrict yourself to just those books marked 'Witchcraft'. Look at country life, seasonal festivals, ancient religions, local customs and sacred places. As you read, jot down in your Book of Illuminations those facts, poems, ideas and odd bits of lore and folk magic that interest you so that you can come back to them, try them out and really understand them as your knowledge grows.

Exercises

Read the chapter a couple of times and note the things which most seem to click with you. If you are going to follow the thirteen lessons month by month you will have to choose a day on which to start, preferably that after a new moon. Buy a large A4 notebook and a hardback spring-clip file to keep your pages in. You can decorate the cover, for this will become your personal Book of Illumination, so find a secret place to keep it in so that honest accounts of dreams, ideas, wishes and discoveries can be entered without fear of their being read by others. Later on, you will need to enter details of spells you have worked, indications about divinations and their outcome, and information on all sorts of things.

Go to the children's section of your library or bookshop and see what they have on Comparative Religion. You need basic information to understand what people believe, ordinary Catholic or Anglican Christians, Quakers, Methodists and some of the other world faiths, like Buddhism, Hinduism, Judaism, Shinto, Islam and any others which interest you. You will also come across Greek, Roman and Egyptian religions from the ancient world, and they have close bearings on some aspects of modern paganism.

Become really nosy and curious about where you live, why it is there, what was there before. Find out what is sacred or special in the area, the origin of the place name. If you have contact with any old people, your grandparents or other elderly folk, ask them about how the place used to be, any local celebrations or curious customs. Look hard at things, as suggested in this chapter, especially out of doors. Watch the moon growing and changing her position in the sky, night by night, when the sky is clear. Go and feel the atmosphere at the nearest sacred place. How does it feel different?

Read up on the farming year, the old agricultural practices and the seasonal work. Find out if there is a local museum with old tools and kitchen equipment, or layouts of traditional cottages. Try to get the feel of a cruder, simpler past, and the people of long ago.

Ask yourself questions about what you *know* about witchcraft, what you believe it to be like, what it can do for you, and what you can offer to the Craft in return. Compare what you have read in books about pagan ideas with what you are finding out about the lives of people in earlier times. Write down notes on all you discover on the first pages of your Book of Illumination.

Here are a few books to get you going:

Doreen Valiente, *Witchcraft for Tomorrow* (Robert Hale)
Starhawk, *The Spiral Dance* (Harper and Row, USA)
Prudence Jones and Caitlín Matthews, *Voices from the Circle* (Aquarian)
Marian Green, *The Gentle Arts of Aquarian Magic* (Aquarian)

2.

MEETING THE GODDESS AND GOD OF THE WITCHES

I am that soundless, boundless, bitter sea.
All tides are mine, and answer unto me.
Tides of the airs, tides of the inner earth,
The secret, silent tides of death and birth.
Tides of men's souls, and dreams, and destiny –
Isis Veiled, and Ea, Binah, Ge . . .

Dion Fortune: *The Sea Priestess*

The pagan religion of witchcraft is one in which each seeker sets out on a personal inner quest to meet and communicate directly with various aspects of the goddess or god of their chosen tradition. It is not a faith, so 'belief' in invisible deities, and orthodox dogma should have no part in the matter.

In this chapter I will try to set out some of the widely held ideas about the Goddess and about her consort, the Sun God, so that you can make your own choices as to whether they have any validity for you, if their attributes appeal to you, or if you feel drawn towards their myths or their symbols. No one, inside the Craft, would ever insist that someone has to accept these Great Ones in a particular form, or that they have to be worshipped in only one way. The seasonal festivals celebrated by coven witches often act out the life cycles of the Goddess in her various guises, and her Son/Lover. In some cases the High Priestess and the High Priest raise their own consciousness to become united with these deities, and so perceive them and show them to the rest of the coven in a very intimate way. Those who follow the Old Ways alone will come to know each aspect as a real being, as a friend and guide.

What is said about the nature of the Old Ones by someone other than yourself can only ever be their own personal description, just as another person may try to describe a piece of

music or the flavour of a rare delicacy to someone who has
sampled neither. Words are inadequate, and can at best only be
vague impressions of what can often be a very deep and
emotional experience. Because there is no 'bible' of witchcraft,
there is no single source of inherited myths and religious stories,
shared by all neo-pagans. It is felt that the gods are continuing
to live out their own lives, and so with each cycle of the Earth
among the stars, there will be a slightly different version of their
story. The pagan gods and goddesses are not fixed and
completed beings, whose will is immutable and whose actions
are distant. All of them are immanent, close to us, accessible.
If we make the effort of prayer, invocation or magic, we will be
able to perceive them, in a way we can actually comprehend,
seeing them as great beings of power. All that can really be
taught is the simple ways in which this meeting, on another
level of our being, can be brought about, so that seekers can see
for themselves how that religious relationship will best fit into
their own concepts and philosophy.

Firstly, though, we do need to understand something about
the eternal, ever-changing, many-faceted and varied guises in
which the Great Mother and the Sky God are perceived among
those who try to walk in their ways. The Goddess is an undying,
threefold being, who can be understood as our original star-
born Mother. She is commonly associated with the planet
Earth, as Mother Nature, the Earth Goddess, Gaia, the First
Parent, self-fertile, bearer of all living creatures, human,
animal, and often all plants and other sentient life forms. We
know that all living things *are* born of the Earth, made of its
substance, taken in with food and water. We know, too, that
the Earth is a small scrap of star stuff, captured by the nearest
star, our Sun, so our own original heritage is from the stars, at
the birth of creation.

The Goddess in many of her pagan pantheons is also the
Moon Goddess, triple-faced and triple-phased. The young
Moon Maiden, child sweetheart, beloved mistress, growing
daughter of the night, is her waxing form. Full-bellied Moon
Mother, full-blown rose of light, travellers' joy, guide and
companion on the magical paths, she leads our monthly revels.
In her waning phase, she is the dark-visaged hag deep-steeped
in wisdom, crotchety and sharp, but she is the giver of
knowledge to those who will face her in the darkness, and as a
dutiful grandchild ask for help. The Moon Goddess also has a

hidden face, at the dark of the moon, when the night sky is empty and the light of the stars alone illumines the wild places. This aspect of her you will need to discover for yourself, man or woman, for this is part of the Mystery of moon magic, and is not spoken of in words.

The Goddess is also Ocean, the great sea from which arose the evolving forms of life, third mother to us human beings. The first mother is Earth, the second the moon awakening mind, and the third mother, all the sacred waters, from spring and pool, to lake and river, to mighty sea and moon-led power of the tides. Those who become her children will find her in all her aspects, alive in wild places, and in those magic rings, circles out of time, between the worlds, created by ritual and controlled desire.

The Goddess is nameless, yet she has many names in many lands and pantheons. If you examine their mystery you will find not names but titles, attributes, 'job descriptions', even, spelled out in many tongues. The Goddess is the Ruler of Change, of Times and Tides, and as such she is the Mistress of Magic, for that is 'the art of causing, controlling and shaping change, in this world and the inner worlds'. She is the Giver of Oracles, for nearly all the ancient sacred centres had their sybil, or oracular priestess, working under the thrall of the Goddess to offer wisdom to those who came to ask. She is the Birth-Bringer, the Death-Taker and the Rebirth-Giver also. She is the Initiator of the magician, the Inspirer of poets, who have drunk from her magic cauldron or heard her singing in the light of dawn. She is the Enchantress, the Spell-Weaver, the Charmer and Binder, the Measurer of Life's Thread and She Who Cuts the Thread. She is Our Lady in Darkness, ruler of the Underworld, the Otherworld, Queen of the Dead and the Unborn. She is the Healer and Restorer, and she redeems our forgotten, childlike selves, if we call upon her.

If you look at the names applied to her in the ritual invocation at the head of this chapter (taken from one of Dion Fortune's novels, *The Sea Priestess*), you will see several names attributed to the Great Goddess. Isis, she who rules the pantheon of gods and goddesses of ancient Egypt, as Isis Veiled, the Queen of Nature. The name Isis, *Aset* in Egyptian, means 'Throne', so she represents the 'seat of power', the base, the structure of that which is worshipped. Ea is the Mother of Time, Soul of Space, Oldest of the Old. Binah, the dark

Mother of All, the great sea, the female principle, *yin*. Ge is the sphere of the Earth, root of such words as 'geology' – the science of rocks; 'geography' – mapping the Earth; 'geomancy' – a magical form of divination whose symbols are drawn in the earth. None of these sacred titles is a 'name'.

Similarly, if you start to look for images you will find many, in every culture, apart from Islam in which all depictions are forbidden. You will discover paintings, carvings, embroideries, rock pictures, statues, pottery figures, even huge earthworks, like that at Silbury Hill in the South of England, depicting or symbolising the Great Goddess in her many guises, or displaying her various traditional symbols. From the great image of the moon in the sky, which is also her symbol (for she is not the physical mass of the moon), to the tides which it creates within the mighty oceans and smallest rivers, to the rising waters of springs: the seasons of the Earth, and the substance of the Earth beneath our feet, on which we have our homes and being, all these are parts of her. All are sacred, and held as holy in her name. All have power which we may draw upon, once we gain the key which unlocks her secret wisdom.

The Goddess has to be invoked, that is, called up in the *imagination* by using poetic description and symbols associated with the aspect which you seek to contact. If you are new to this idea, keep it simple. Use a prayer or description from a classical source, when you are in a quiet place. It is usually best out of doors, and simply standing beside a river, in a garden or any natural setting, where you feel at peace and free. Read the words, or imagine the image, then close your eyes and relax and see what happens. Here is a description taken from Apuleius' story *The Golden Ass* in which the hero, Lucius, invokes the Goddess and . . .

> *I had scarcely closed my eyes before the apparition of a woman began to rise from the middle of the sea with so lovely a face that the gods themselves would have fallen down in adoration of it. First the head, then the whole shining body gradually emerged and stood before me, poised on the surface of the waves . . . Her long thick hair fell in tapering ringlets on her lovely neck, and was crowned with an intricate chaplet, woven of every kind of flower. Just above her brow shone a round disc, like a mirror, or the bright face of the moon, which told me who she was. Her many-coloured robe was of finest linen . . . and along the hem was a bordure of flowers and fruit. . . . The deep black*

lustre of her mantle, slung across her body from the right hip to the left shoulder and caught into a great knot, was embroidered with glittering stars . . . and in the middle beamed a full and fiery moon . . . All the perfumes of Arabia floated into my nostrils as the Goddess deigned to address me: 'You see me here, Lucius, in answer to your prayer. I am Nature, the Universal Mother, mistress of all the elements, primordial child of time, sovereign of all things spiritual, queen of the dead, queen also of the immortals, the single manifestation of all gods and goddesses that are. My gesture governs the shining heights of Heaven, the wholesome sea breezes, the lamentable silences of the land below. Though I am worshipped in many aspects, known by countless names, and propitiated with all manner of different rites, yet the whole round Earth venerates me.'

This fragment of a magical book, of adventure, folly, sacrifice and communion with the Goddess, in which Lucius is transformed into a donkey until the Goddess frees him and makes him her priest, contains the very essence of pagan worship and the invocation of Isis very powerfully demonstrates the kind of image words can conjure up. Similar esoteric verses, prayers and invocations will be found in the works of many poets, ancient writers, priests of the old religions which predate Christianity, including the Bible. The Song of Solomon contains beautiful love poems dedicated to Sophia, the Goddess of Wisdom, describing her face in terms of flowers, her breasts as white deer, feeding among lilies. Do not overlook this book because it seems to reject the power of the wise one. In fact both the Old and New Testaments contain much magical and pagan information, if you are willing to search it out.

The God of the Witches is also many-faceted, being symbolised by the sun in the sky, and, because of the changes that the turning seasons bring, he is an evolving deity too. He is also depicted surprising frequently as having horns or, in Britain and France, the antlers of a great stag. Like the Goddess, he has many titles, which often refer to his being a Horned God; Herne, or Cernunnos, or Pan, that archetypal half-man, half-beast, ruler of wild creatures in the ancient forests.

Like the Goddess, he has three aspects. His hairy legs and hoofs link him with the animal kingdom, as their guardian and shepherd; his human body from the waist up, containing his human heart, shows that he can feel for the humankind in his care, and is their Lord of Life. His noble brow, dark, thoughtful eyes sparkling with humour, and above those the lordly antlers, show he is Divine, in his own right. These antlers are the symbols of the sun's rays, of the power of Light, of co-creation, and like the points on the earthly king's golden crown, they signify royalty. The God of the pagans walks in three worlds: the lowly land of all beasts, wild and tame, with their simplicity; the man-made realms and agricultural/industrial complexes, for he has always been the Magical Smith, the Maker and Designer: and above these he is the Divine Sky Father.

In the story of the Goddess and the God which may form the underlying pattern of the pagan cycles of celebrations, the God is born of the Lady in midwinter and, like all nameless gods, is known as 'Mabon, son of Modron,' literally 'Son, son of the Mother,' in Welsh. It is a familiar idea, found in many faiths world wide, of a magical son born in humble circumstances to a mother who does not appear to have a husband. How can she? For the God is also his own father, loving his mother, becoming her husband, and yet she outlives him. The God is a cyclic being, closely related to the greenery of the land, being born in winter dark, growing through the days of spring, coming to his full strength, with the sun above, at midsummer, and learning of his impending sacrifice at harvest. Here he is cut down, willing victim to the reaper's blade, offering his seed as grain to sustain the people as autumn chills the land. Dead, he is mourned by the Goddess, his widow, who never dies or deserts her children. In the dark months of winter she renews her youth, casting off the face of the hag, and regains her beauty, ready to encounter the young lord in spring.

It is these Mysteries, that of the dying, sacrificed God and the undying, changing Goddess, which form the foundation of pagan worship. The seasonal festivals act out the life cycles of these First Parents, their magical birth, growth, wooing, loving, fulfilment and departure to the Underworld, beyond our knowledge.

Although each changes, both the God and Goddess of the witches are immanent; they can be approached for prayer or consolation, for guidance or for healing. It is through this very personal interrelationship that true paganism is expressed. You will come to see whichever aspects of these Old Ones you most need to help you. By regularly seeking them out in the silent places of your heart and in the natural places of the world, you will get to know them as if they were friends, parents, lovers, teachers, healers or wise old guides throughout your life. Because they are above all agents of change, how you see them, in dreams, meditations and rituals, will reflect what you expect to see. Their substance is not of this world, immutable and fixed, but a plastic, astral substance which can appear in many shapes or characteristics. If you ask to see them as they *are*, perhaps you will see only light, or feel power, or fire – only you can discover that. It is because they have many attributes, evolved through humanity's long childhood, and many faces, names, associations and powers that it is important to consider the concept expressed by Dion Fortune, that 'All Gods are One God, and all Goddesses are One Goddess, and there is One Initiator.' She is only echoing earlier words put into the mouth of Isis by Apuleius, writing 1800 years before.

This multiplicity of deities can seem confusing to some people, unless the foregoing is taken into consideration. You are dealing with a variety of aspects, personified *by people* as many gods and goddesses, but just as the Roman Catholics have many saints, all being credited with their own life stories, martyrdoms and specialities, so did the earlier pagans see their own deities. Underlying both traditions is the concept of a Creator or, to the magical folk, an Initiator, by whose power those lesser, more tangible and approachable saints, gods or angelic beings come into existence.

Most pagans do not reject the concept of a creative or generative force, shining as light through the beings of the gods and goddesses, but comprehend it as something beyond, something too ephemeral to define. You will find references to 'Illumination' or 'Enlightenment', 'Seeing the Light', and the ecstasy of 'At-Onement' or 'Unity with All Creation' which occurs during mystical experiences. This is an altogether higher experience than those commonly undergone during rituals, although such work can lead very ordinary people to have some extraordinary visions and inner awakenings, even if such transcendental happenings are not sought or expected.

Here is a fictional character's response to encountering one of the aspects of the Lord of the Wild, taken from what some people might think is a strange source, a children's story book, *The Wind in the Willows* by Kenneth Grahame. Some of the animal characters are looking for the otter's child and are led to an island:

In silence they landed, and pushed through the blossom and scented herbage . . . till they stood on a little lawn of marvellous green, set round with Nature's own orchard trees – crab apple, wild cherry and sloe. 'This is the place of my song-dream, the place the music played to me,' whispered the Rat, as if in a trance, 'Here in this holy place, here if anywhere, surely we shall find Him!'

Then suddenly the Mole felt a great Awe fall upon him . . . it was no panic terror – indeed he felt wonderfully at peace and happy – but it was an awe that smote and held him . . . And still there was silence in the populous bird-haunted branches; . . . and still the light grew and grew . . . The summons seemed still dominant and imperious. He might not refuse were Death himself waiting to strike him instantly, once he had looked on things . . . rightly kept hidden. Trembling he obeyed . . . and then in that utter clearness of the imminent dawn, whilst Nature flushed with incredible colour . . . he looked in the eyes of the Friend and Helper; he saw the backward sweep of the curved horns, gleaming in the growing daylight; saw the stern, hooked nose between the kindly eyes that were looking down on them humorously, while the bearded mouth broke into a half-smile at the corners; saw the rippling muscles on the arm that lay across the broad chest, the long supple hand still holding the pan-pipes only just fallen away from the still parted lips; saw the splendid curves of the shaggy limbs disposed in majestic ease on the sward; saw, last of all, nestling between his very hooves, . . . the little round form of the baby otter . . .

Then the two animals, crouching to the earth, bowed their heads and did worship.

Sudden and magnificent, the sun's golden disc showed itself over the horizon, and the first rays, shooting across the level water meadows, dazzled them. When they were able to look once more, the Vision had vanished, and the air was full of the carol of birds that hailed the dawn.

The whole passage, from the chapter 'Piper at the Gates of Dawn', is well worth reading thoroughly and its symbolism and powerful images used for meditation. Similarly beautiful invocations of Pan are to be found in the magical invocations of Aleister Crowley, the pagan poems of Doreen Valiente and in the novels of Dion Fortune, especially *The Goatfoot God*. You will need to seek out those depictions, invocations and images which most closely call to your inner vision the form of the Great God of Nature, the Lord of the Wild or the Horned Hunter, antler-crowned, who leads his mysterious pack of hounds across the sky, harbinger of storms or tempests.

These are not tame powers, however; neither God nor Goddess needs to be seen in the same context as gentle Jesus, meek and mild. Doreen Valiente conjures up the experience in the words of part of her poem, *Invocation to the Horned God*:

Come, O come, to the heartbeat's drum!
Come to us who gather below, When the broad white moon is climbing slow,
Through the stars to the heaven's height. We hear thy hooves on the wind of night!
As black tree branches shake and sigh, By joy and terror we know thee nigh.
We speak the spell thy power unlocks, At solstice, sabbat and equinox,
Word of virtue, the veil to rend, From primal dawn to the wide world's end.

It is the combined feeling of excitement and sacredness which shows to neo-pagans that their God and Goddess are in some way present in rituals or in the celebration of festivals, many of which enact their life story. The ideas which you may explore for their validity for yourself include the most widely accepted concepts about the Mighty Ones. First, you need to consider the multiplicity of their natures, both Male and Female, Mother and Father, Immanent and yet Holy. You need to be aware that many pagans accept the idea of a Creative Spirit, Initiator, First Emanation from the void. You also need to be aware that the principle of reincarnation is common among pagans and witches, who hold that every living creature has an immortal spirit which, evolving as it goes, lives through many lives.

Some of the themes of meditations and self-explorations may well lead you to recall your previous lives, in other 'selves', and the knowledge you had then, the relationships and long-lasting bonds of love or hate which re-emerge in this life to bring joy or pain. Within this concept of eternal and evolutionary life is the concept of *karma*, an Eastern term meaning not just 'fate' or 'destiny' but an interlinked chain of action and response in our human affairs. It is not a simple 'knock for knock' arrangement tying two parties into continuing conflict, but a theory which suggests that good actions will lead to pleasure and those which are harmful, to yourself or others, will hold you back by limiting your freedom. Each action you make in the world affects the entire universe. If your action is basically evolutionary, you will move a fraction forward; if it prevents evolution, then you will suffer the consequences. It is for this reason that the skills of real magic are only bestowed, by the Goddess, on these who can handle the power with care.

Love, honour, respect and personal responsibility are among the watchwords of most successful witches and magicians. You have to learn that even to offer healing, unasked, can be a harmful act, for it interferes with the life pattern of another human being. If someone is 'miraculously healed' without learning from the experience, it will have to be repeated, and if you tried to heal them, then perhaps you will suffer some illness. Most of the traditional sorts of spells the old witches were asked for were those to make people fall in love with the witch's client, or to break up marriages, or grant power to those who were not ready to handle it. Today most of those sorts of requests would be met with a long counselling session, perhaps using a form of divination to help the client sort out his or her own love life. To win love you have to deserve it by being a lovable person – there is no other way!

Spells and magic will not lead to power or riches or fame unless the one who seeks such rewards is ready and capable of handling these, and all of them have their price. To be powerful, in any field, means that you are also controlled and responsible, sensible and caring. To have wealth implies that you have earned it, not stolen or conned it out of its rightful owner. There are many things which witches possess which are incredibly valuable, yet have no monetary price, nor can they be bought or stolen. These include peace of mind; harmony and joy in their relationships, both earthly and with the gods; success in their chosen fields of life, perhaps without the added burden of fame; a wisdom and inner knowledge which will answer most of life's problems, and an enduring patience which will see them through the rough patches. Most of the ordinary standards by which success is measured do not apply, but you can see by the light in their eyes rather than the money in the bank how well they are doing in the Game of Life!

Although covens do have High Priestesses and High Priests who may well have progressed through stages and degrees set by their Tradition, the direct communion with the Old Ones will make all sincere seekers into their own priesthood. Having a qualification of some sort has not always been a necessity to this sacred calling. The oracles are chosen by the Goddess, who speaks through them, but without diminishing their awareness or entrancing their minds, a very different concept to that of mediumship, or channelling, as it is sometimes called these days. Those who walk in the Old Ways may well find that in verse and ritual, in song and dance the Great Ones can indicate their will through those who are dedicated to their wisdom.

Another valuable task certainly carried out by witches of old, as they served their communities, was that called, in the Celtic Church, 'Soul Friends'. These people, men and women, were respected for the way they lived their lives and would be freely consulted by anyone in trouble, of heart, mind or spirit. It was possible to discuss spiritual or emotional matters with them, in a lonely grove or quiet garden. There was no offering of forgiveness by an unsanctified priesthood, but gentle comfort, support or guidance. All these things have been sadly neglected in our hurried world. To be able to turn to a wise friend, whose views would be impartial yet caring could go a long way to easing the spiritual deprivation of our towns and cities. Soul Friends were companions of children, who might tell of rough treatment by their elders; or of single women deserted by their menfolk yet trying to rear children alone. They helped the elderly, slowly walking to the gates of death, yet comforted and guided by those wise in such matters. Perhaps the witches of the New Age will restore such a sacred calling to their repertoire, and be willing to listen and advise both pagans and others who seek such consolation.

You cannot be forced to believe anything, but you can allow your own inner being, your own eternal, reincarnating (if you accept it does) spirit to show you what is truth in the matter of religious action or faith. Seek to understand, rejecting nothing until you have really tried to comprehend. This goes just as much for aspects of the faith you may be trying to exchange for pagan philosophies and practices, for the seeds of much valuable learning may be hidden in holy books, as well as bigotry, nonsense and out-of-date ideas. Read for the poetry, the words in praise of deity, the actions of the satisfied heart and awakened spirit. Examine the words and works of any pagans or witches you come across. Would you really like to be like them, hold their world views, their attitudes, biases and concepts of deity, without bending your own truly held beliefs? No true religion will suppress debate, honest examination of its sacred texts, or discussion of its tenets by any seeker who is trying to understand. The more rules and restrictions, the more hollow the teaching and empty the lore. The witches hold one sentence as their Law: 'An it harm none, do what ye will.' 'None' in this case implies everyone and everything! 'An' in old English means 'In order that' and 'will' is your soul's own true will, not the whim of the moment.

Another underlying principle of the paganism of witchcraft is the idea that every individual contains a spark of the Creator, manifested as both God and Goddess inside each of us. Those who take up the duties as a New Age priest or priestess will eventually learn, directly from those deities within, how to handle their powers, speak with their voices, bless with their benediction. It is not something which can be expressed in a book, but has to be learned patiently, by personal dedication and commitment to that path. It is not an easy option, either, for to serve the Creative Principle is a very hard, heavy and enduring task which, once taken up, cannot be set aside for human reasons. If you work through the exercises, make the effort required to attune yourself with the powers of Nature, interact with the God and Goddess as they may appear to you in dreams and visions then eventually their twin powers within you will awaken.

Some Traditions teach only of either the God or Goddess within, but in reality, because our immortal, reincarnating spirits may be either male or female, there dwells deep within the nature of both sexes. When this is awoken our understanding of relationships, friendships, love and passion is increased immeasurably. It is by working with the God *and* Goddess within that we may gain much of our magical power, and alongside that the will to control it and the responsibility to use it properly. If you look at the earlier part of this chapter, you will see which are the main attributes of the God and Goddess as they exist and are available to everyone, and then you may be able to choose those aspects which you most need to invoke in yourself, using your inner God/Goddess force to do this. Gradually you will learn the ancient art of symbolism and magic, wherein a certain sign, number, colour, tree or flower may represent that which you wish to contact, and by its ritual use, or even mental imagination, you will be able to ask clearly for specific help, and receive just that. The rituals and charms, the talismans and spells of the Old Ones were much less sophisticated than the ones some magically-minded witches use today. Both sorts work, but a return to the older, simpler and more natural methods will do no harm.

Exercises

You may already be encountering difficulties because you are choosing to redirect your life, and walk an uncommon path, but if you are really intent on walking the Old Way you will need to persevere.

Again, the second Moon requires you to carry on research as well as looking at what is going on in the community around you. Look at every tree you see, take every opportunity to witness or join in local well-dressing, bonfire processions or morris dances. They all contain hidden jewels of our forgotten pagan heritage. Also find time to be quiet every day, meditating if you know how, or at least mulling over what you have read, what you have written in your Book of Illumination, and all the ideas flitting like bats through your mind, by day and night.

Here are some more things to do in your second Moon of training. Consider what it means to have a Goddess and a God with many forms. Also read and think hard about religious experience, what it should do or may have done for you in the past. What would you consider a mystical experience to be like?

Divide one page of your Book of Illumination into two columns and write 'The Goddess' at the top of one column, and 'The God' at the top of the other. Begin by writing in each pairs of names, attributes, symbols or titles, matching the Goddess as Moon with the God as Sun, for example. Sometimes you have three Goddess attributes and only one God name, but you will gradually find balances. You should be able to continue this list through several pages, especially if you take some of the classical deities as well as the local ones.

Sit silently with your eyes closed, relax and then ask the Goddess to show herself to you. See what happens after a few minutes, and write it in your Book. On another occasion ask for the God to appear, and again record what you see or experience. Then ask to see them both.

Draw a large circle (round a plate) and enter the Festivals, taking the top to be north. In segments, add symbols, colours, flowers and all the other things you personally associate with each feast. If you don't know very much yet, rather than copying from this book, add more after each festival passes.

Look at poetry, more or less at random, in bookshops or the library. Try to devise your own brief invocations for the elements that surround your circle. Work with the basic powers rather than elaborate god-names which you may not fully understand. Try to open up your emotions rather than treating this as an intellectual exercise.

Walk about out of doors and visit somewhere that you would consider sacred, be it religious site, highest local hilltop, ancient monument, old tree or spring of fresh water. Try to discover how and why it feels different to any similar 'non-sacred' place. Relax with your eyes closed and stretch your senses.

Here are a selection of books to look out for:

Robert Graves, *The White Goddess* (Faber)
Caitlín Matthews, *The Elements of the Goddess* (Element Books)
Miranda Green, *The Gods of the Celts* (Alan Sutton)
William James, *Varieties of Religious Experience* (Penguin)
Marian Green, *A Harvest of Festivals* (Longman, out of print)

Don't expect any of these books to be a very easy read, nor do any of them explain exactly about the Old Village Witch or Cunning Man because there is very little written about them, except as parts of learned studies by folklorists, but they are a treasure house of useful ideas.

3.

THE SACRED CYCLES

To every thing there is a season, and a time to every purpose under heaven: a time to be born, a time to die; a time to plant, and a time to reap; a time to kill, and a time to heal; . . . a time to weep, and a time to laugh; a time to mourn, and a time to dance; . . . a time to keep, and a time to cast away; . . . a time to keep silence, and a time to speak; a time to love, and a time to hate; a time of war, and a time of peace.

Old Testament; Ecclesiastes 3

The land on which we live is subject to the cycles of the seasons. To our ancestors every part of the year had its tasks, its unrewarded efforts and its harvests, its times of dearth and glut, success and failure, plenty or famine. What happened to the crops or the fertility of the livestock was seen to be partly in the hands of the farmers with their inherited wisdom, and partly in the gift of the Earth Mother. It is for this reason that, from the earliest known religious activities of humankind upon Earth, offerings, rituals, celebrations and acts of propitiation seem to have been made in her name.

Most of the oldest identifiable religious objects appear to be in the form of fat women, usually described by archaeologists and others as primitive Earth Mother figures, or Mother Goddess statues. As the understanding of the varied nature of the Goddess evolved these became more elaborate, showing not just the fat belly and ample breasts, but beautiful headdresses, armlets which are sometimes snakes, flounced skirts or elegant necklaces and breast ornaments. All over the world such ancient representations are to be found, echoing the most advanced art forms of their age. Some are painted on cave walls or roofs, some are carved from soft stone, moulded in clay, woven from reeds, cast from precious metals and decorated with jewels. Each individually expresses the artist's prayer, of thanksgiving or supplication, or worship of a specific aspect of the Great Goddess, as seen in his or her age.

Recent ideas about ancient structures, mounds, earthworks, 'burial mounds' and reshapings of the landscape seem to indicate that even on this vast scale, effigies of a Mother Goddess, Birth-Giver, Life-Taker, have been set out among the hills. Many of these artificial constructions seem to echo the shape of the womb, or the pregnant and fecund belly of she who brings forth young. Many of the shapes associated with the Goddess from earliest times include circles, holes, the 'vesica piscis', or the crescent of the moon's shifting outline. Serpents and many flowers appear as symbols of the life force of the First Mother, and many springs, wells and fountains are sacred to her power.

Similarly, there are many upright pillar stones, phallic totem poles, carvings of the sun, or windows in structures where the rising light of the sun can send its fertilising ray deep into the dark heart of the Goddess-shaped long barrow, symbolically uniting the sky with the Earth. Here the God as the sunlight and the Goddess as the earthwork, at a very precise moment in the turning year, come together, magically ensuring fertility and the return of the spring. Many of the circles of standing stones have been found to align with specific sunrises or sunsets, or the appearance of the moon on the horizon. We have had to wait until computer graphics systems were developed before these ancient, mathematically accurate layouts of markers could be understood for what they teach us about the wisdom of our ancestors. Stones, ditches, mounds, cuts in the horizon, straight and curved trackways, canals and pools, all have been deliberately engineered by ancient priests or scientists, to act as accurate calendars or time markers.

Time's passage was always of importance to early people. Stone Age bone carvings track the pattern of the moon's face through the sky in its twenty-nine-day passage from new to new again. It is likely that first tall poles and then heavy stones were carefully set to show the relationship between the sun and the seasons. Even before the time when the sowing of seeds introduced the very beginnings of agriculture, the passing seasons provoked interest and perhaps wonder in the early peoples of Britain and Europe. Much scientific research has been centred on the calendar-like circles of stones, ignoring the

fact that farmers then, as now, sowed seed when their own fields
were dry and warm enough to allow them to flourish. Crops are
harvested when they are ripe, or in order to save them from
rough weather, not because some great stone sundial has
marked out a particular day. Even the breeding of livestock has
to be left to their own inclinations, when the ewes, cows or
mares are receptive. A sunbeam falling on a particular spot in a
sacred courtyard will not make the rams, stallions and bulls
more willing. It might work in reverse, however; the farmers
saw when their livestock mated and noted the time against these
calendar-clocks, or recorded in some simple way where the sun
rose when the soil was ready for sowing, or how the moon shone
at harvest time.

This need for the organisation and activities of the people to
follow the phases of Nature is largely overlooked now. Just as
the monks of the early Church invented clocks and set fixed
dates for their saints' days, regulating the lives of all the people,
so the modern witches often meet by the clock or the calendar
instead of by the tides of the Earth Goddess and her Sky Lord.
It is important to become aware of the actual phases of the
moon, not by looking at a watch dial or printed poster on the
wall, but by making the effort to go outside in the evening and
look for the moon herself. It is worth rising early and seeing
where and when the sun rises, for he too traces a different path
along the horizon, from the north in summer to the south in
winter.

If you are working alone, or with a friend or two, in the old
manner, it will be easier for you to hold your celebration or
meditation on the night of the new or full moon, at an equinox
or solstice, or the first day after the snowdrops bloom in your
winter garden.

Pre-Christian people in Europe worked out the passage of
time in moon phases and because of this they probably had a
moon-number of great festivals. The oldest seem to be the
beginning of winter, the middle of winter and the end of winter.
In summer they would probably be too busy to find time to
gather and celebrate, working from dawn to dusk, hay making,
weeding, tending livestock, shearing the sheep, then reaping
the corn and stooking it, and carrying it into the barns and
threshing out the grain. Then there would be the gathering of
wild and cultivated fruits and vegetables and fungi to be stored
for the 'hungry gap' of the winter. In autumn, the beasts would

be brought in from the hills and woods and some slaughtered and salted down for the winter. Fat would be rendered both for eating and to burn as lamp oil. At each change of occupation it would be Nature herself who would instruct the people what to do. Gradually several overlapping patterns began to emerge, and it is from the cycles of the life of the land and the farm stock, and the magical lives of the Goddess and the God, that some of the festivals which are celebrated by modern pagans began to develop.

I think that if some of the witches of today thought more about the actual workings of Nature and less of book-bound, set knowledge, they would gain more power in their magics, more joy in their celebrations, and a greater sense of unity with their ancestors and the ancient faith they aim to follow. It was, after all, the Church that fixed the dates of the old Festivals, and it is from that restrictive form of belief that most of them are trying to untangle themselves! This is especially true at the end of the twentieth century, when it seems that great changes are occurring in our weather systems; spring is coming earlier in the south of Britain, with more winter rain, high winds and overflowing waterways.

Nature marked out the turning seasons with a series of alternating White and Green harvests, and it was from these that the original nine feasts came to be established. You don't have to take my word for it, but look out of your window, observe and take note of those outdoor happenings which presage every change of season.

All over the world, the Goddess is seen or known as the White Goddess. White flowers, clothes or offerings have always been associated with her, from the snowy-white icefields of the north, to the white-hot burning deserts on the equator; to the southern lands, lying under the Long White Cloud. We see it today in the white dresses of brides at their marriage, when the young lady, for that day, represents the Goddess to her husband; in the white costumes, with their bells, ribbons and flowers, of the Morris Men, 'Mary's Men', dancing in honour of the White Goddess. Even in India, a land where white is a colour of mourning, it is into the hands of the Goddess of Death, with her white face, that the departed soul will travel.

The White harvests represent stages in the lives of the Goddess and the God, defined at a moment when a certain kind of power was to be felt, and perhaps shared with the people.

The 'green' festivals are set around the solar agricultural dates
of the Equinoxes and Solstices. The old rites were simple and
largely intuitive affairs, when a whole village or community
would come together to act out part of the Old Ones' story, to
renew the bonds of dedication to the Lord and Lady, and those
ties of kinship within the human relationships, or forge new
ones. There was no priest to intercede between the people and
their deities, for even in the pre-Christian Celtic era when the
Druids held sway, they seemed to have acted more as guides or
masters of ceremonies than controllers of the ritual. Everyone in
the community probably made a small offering, asked a boon,
or offered prayers of thanksgiving, as appropriate to the season.
If there was speech, it was from the heart and Goddess-given
inspiration rather than set-piece sermons or regulated
supplications. As most such celebrations were carried out in
fields or woods or sacred circles of standing stones, it is likely
that much of the action was mime, just as today's mumming
plays enact the story of Life and Death, Summer and Winter,
with a variety of local characters depicted. Song and dance too
would have played a part in such gatherings, with music,
drumming and probably the playing of games like those
country children still play. Often those who acted out the
characters of the story of the Old Ones would be chosen by lot,
with symbols baked into a cake, or hidden in a bag. This
allowed the God or Goddess to cast his or her part without the
intervention of human will. When this method of choosing the
parts for a ritual or celebration is used, those so chosen play
their parts far better than might be imagined, even if they do not
exactly fit the archetype they portray.

Starting at the beginning of the Celtic year, around the end of
October in the modern calendar, when the first hard frost
whitened the grass, shrivelled any greenstuff and iced over a
shallow puddle, the community began their preparations for
winter. Cattle and pigs and sheep which had roamed the
unfenced fells, moors or woodland would be brought back to the
farmyards or perhaps one of the great earthworks which dot the
southern hilltops. It would be a great round-up and time for
sorting out the stock. Some would be selected to be killed as,
before the times of extensive haymaking and the production of
winter feed, not all could be expected to survive through the
winter months. Pigs would be salted into ham and bacon, but a
great feast of those parts which could not be preserved would be

eaten. The White harvest of this time would be fat and hides and fleeces, all vital to see the people through the winter.

Next, as the nights grew longer and the air colder, the people, less sure than we are today that the warmth of spring actually would return, made many spells and enchantments to call back the sun from his long journey into night. On the darkest night, at what is now called the Winter Solstice, when the whole community huddled round the blazing yule log, the mysterious Star Child, Son of the Goddess, the Mabon, was born. As Sun God, he stood for the return of the Light but there was doubt until, by a few minutes a day, the nights began to shorten. It is for this reason that the births of the Christ Child and his predecessor, Mithras, both sacrificial gods born in a cave or stable, are celebrated on 25th December. That was the day when the Wise Ones could announce that the magic had worked, that the bonfires on the hilltops, the offerings of greenery and red berries, the decking of the houses and the giving of gifts, especially to children, had brought a return of the Light.

There would then be a period of real rejoicing with the best of the stored foods being brought out, the fatted goose prepared for the table, the last sweet apples, dried fruits and nuts brought out in celebration. This was a time of great hardship in many communities, if the grain harvests had been poor or the livestock sickly, yet once the promise of the Star Child, the Child of Hope as he was known in some old villages, had been seen, the entire community would do what they could to celebrate. There were round dances, called originally 'carols', performed in barns or out of doors if it was dry enough, and special songs, some fragments of which are still sung these days, with the words changed to greet a newer Lord. It was the greenery, the holly and the ivy, branches of fir sweet-smelling in the smoky houses, and the magical mistletoe, sacred to the Druids, which enriched this dark time. Those customs are still with us, as well as the dressing of the sacred tree with lights and tinsel. All have pagan roots.

All celebrations have to end and the Yuletide feast was concluded with another day of special activities, called in the Christian calendar Epiphany or Twelfth Night. In that tradition, it is the time when the Wise Men from the East arrived, astrologers following a star and bringing gifts of the Frankincense of Royalty, the Gold of Material Power, and the bitter Myrrh of the Sacrifice to come. This also echoes a Celtic tradition whereby the young man or woman, at about the age of twelve to fourteen years, gained their adult name and status. In the Old Religion it is when the Young God is initiated into the wisdom of the Clan, and receives his name, his magical weapons and instructions for his life. Although this particular festival has been overlooked by witches whose rituals use the eightfold contemporary cycle, instead of the ninefold lunar pagan one, various country customs and village celebrations do recall this end to the midwinter feasts. Even in ordinary houses, it is Twelfth Night when the dried-up remains of the Christmas greenery is thrown on the fire, and the last decorations in homes and churches are taken down and stored away. Out of doors, in places where cider orchards flourish, there is the ritual of Wassailing the trees, by pouring libations and sticking bread or toast soaked in cider in the branches of the apple trees. Shotguns are fired to drive away harm, and songs are sung, 'Here's to thee, Old Apple Tree, much mayst thou bear, Hats full, caps full and great bushel baskets full. Hurrah!'

In some villages other rituals are to be found at about the middle of January, acknowledging the end of the hardest part of winter, and expressing a hope for the future spring. In Shetland there is a Fire Festival at about this time when a replica Viking ship, surrounded by the islanders in home-made Viking costumes carrying flaming torches, is set afire and allowed to drift out to sea. Both a sacrifice of a ship and an offering for calm weather and full fish nets is accomplished at this winter festival of Up-Helly-Aa. The name is supposed to mean 'the days of the holiday are up'.

When the might of winter loosens its grip upon the land and the first white flowers of the snowdrops nod their pale heads above the melting snow and the first royal purple crocuses thrust their elegant cups into the winter air, many pagans celebrate the Festival of the White Goddess as Brigid, Bride or even Lucy, the Light Bringer. The Church has adopted this feast as Candlemas, when Mary was returned to her people, cleansed after the ritual period after the birth of Jesus. The Celtic name for this celebration is *Oimelc*, literally 'ewes' milk', for now, in the warmer parts of the land, the first lambs are born, and a new harvest of ewes' milk is available for them and the people, to whom this was a valuable foodstuff. To celebrate this feast there is a traditional drink called 'lambswool', made from hot wine or cider and water in which the flesh of several roasted or baked apples are heartily mixed. The resulting frothy white drink resembles lambs' wool. Shakespeare writes of 'the roasted crabs hiss in the bowl' and it is the pink-fleshed crab apples rather than the crustacean he is talking about, 'As nightly sings the staring owl, toowhit toowhoo'. Another good old Goddess symbol, sacred from Britain to Athens.

In the villages this Candlemas feast has two aspects. One is the secret womens' Mystery of how the Goddess renews her youth, and all the women deck with their brightest scarves, their most precious ribbons, a chair beside the hearth to welcome the return of the Goddess. Then in darkness, when the men have been allowed to creep into the room, a small figure in a dark cloak arrives. Wreathed in ivy and warmly wrapped, a young maid from the community brings in the first flowers and the new flame. Under her cloak, which one of the older ladies removes, she is dressed in white and green, and carries a dish of early flowers, snowdrops, violets, jasmine or the earliest daffodils. Among the blossoms is a small candle, and from that a candle for every member of the community is lit, set out on the floor. The Goddess, in the guise of this little girl, is welcomed in a blaze of light and grants her blessing on all. Each of the men and women kneel before her, silently asking a gift or practical help in the coming year, and each pledges the work of their hands to the benefit of the people.

As soon as the soil began to warm up and be workable, roughly at the time of the Spring Equinox (about March 21st), seed corn and barley would have been laboriously sown by hand. Among it would be the special ears of corn saved as the corn dolly or kern king, symbol of the potency of the Sun God, sacrificed at harvest-tide. The Church's calendar has Easter at about this time, too. Easter, again named after a Saxon goddess of spring, Eostre, is the only one of the Christian festivals which is decided by the phases of the moon, which is why it moves about. Easter Sunday is the first Sunday after the full moon on or after the Vernal Equinox, which is when the sun enters the sign of Aries. It is the same time as the Jewish Feast of Pesach, or 'Passing Over', when a lamb is slaughtered and eaten in haste, with bitter herbs and cups of red wine. Many of the other European countries derive their names for this festival from 'Pâsques' in French, 'Pask' in Dutch or 'Pasche' in Latin, most of these being taken to mean 'Passion', and relate to the Crucifixion.

Once again the symbols linked with the Easter festival contain many pre-Christian ones. The decorated eggs, found all over Europe, stand in for the rebirth of Nature; the chocolate rabbit is the Goddess's sacred hare in disguise. The Easter bonnets worn at the Easter Parades represent the new sets of clothes worn for the first time as spring unfurls her golden daffodils, and the tufts of pussy willow fur the branches in the hedges. It is a great time of renewal and new beginnings, when life rises refreshed from its sleep through winter's dark. As day and night are seen to be equal, at the Equinox, the whole energy of the sun helps the Earth to dress in her new green gown.

The next sacred flower to mark the passage of time to the country folk is the hawthorn, sweet-scented may blossom. 'Cast not a clout 'til May be out!' the grandparents advised us not so long ago. The May in question is not necessarily the month, but the quickthorn used as a hedge plant until mechanised farming grubbed up these old corridors of natural life. The first green leaves of hawthorn used to be eaten as a spring tonic and are rich in vitamins, so vital after a boring winter diet of salted meat, hard cheese and rough bread. At May Day, the flowering of the hawthorn signals Beltane, the God's Fire, when the animals were set free from their winter quarters. By may-blooming time there would be more grass, and all the people would be ready to celebrate the advancing warmth and outdoor life. The maypole, a phallic symbol, would be raised on many a village green, and the young children would deck it out with flowers and lace it with ribbons, binding together the fertilising sun power from above with the nourishing earth power below. Bonfires would smoulder and the cattle would be cleansed of ticks by being driven through a thick medicinal smoke of burning herbs.

The days continue to lengthen until midsummer, when the hay would be harvested, and long hours of work would be needed to weed and hoe all the crops. Sheep would be sheared, usually between May Day and midsummer, and the womenfolk would set about the long task of spinning the wool. To us urban folk, the summer is a holiday, but to workers in the fields it was the time of greatest effort, for it was vital to ensure that the crops produced as much food as possible. Charms and spells and songs would be sung as the farming community slogged their way through all the heavy, boring yet essential tasks. In some places peat would be cut from the sticky, insect-ridden bogs, allowed to dry and carted back to the villages or farm houses.

At last the days of the corn harvest would begin with all sorts of customs, which even in the days of combine harvesters are still carried out as the last run of grain in each field is gathered in. Harvest Suppers, garlanded heavy horses parading the golden sheaves through the villages, dances and songs recall the much simpler days when the arduous work of the year was brought to fruition. Then the corn dollies were made from the finest ears of corn, woven to the local design, bound with red ribbons. John Barleycorn was dead, long live John Barleycorn.

Michaelmas and the Autumnal Equinox bring the garnering of the fruits of wood and orchard, the saving of pumpkins and all root vegetables – the final Harvest Home, when all the produce is displayed in churches or village halls, demonstrating the success or failure of the year's work. Geese used to be fattened and with their feet dipped in tar and sand to make 'boots' for the journey, marched to markets in the towns to grace the supper tables at Michaelmas.

Once all is again gathered in, the flocks sorted out, and the first winter frosts whiten the ground, the old feast of Hallowe'en comes round again. It is traditionally a time of disguises, games of chance and those which foretell the future with apple peel or by candle light, in dark mirrors. The Goddess is seen here in her wisdom aspect, and it is a time of consulting the First Parents, inviting them to the Great Feast, telling them of the births and deaths, hopes and fears of the year, in the times of speech and of silence.

The God's Story

Within this pattern of harvests and gifts from Mother Nature there runs the story of the God, Son of the Goddess, Great Mother. Born at midwinter, nameless in a lowly place, he grows, each day as a year in his life, until at the hidden feast of Twelfth Night, he becomes a man. In the Old Religion this is the special time, when the young man who stands in for the God at the enactment of the ritual, asks the questions about his heritage, claims his name, his magical tools and receives initiation from his Mother/Grandmother. As he is set free on his own path the Goddess, using her magic of change, becomes the young maiden again.

At the Spring Equinox the God has become the warrior, the Champion of the Goddess, and like such heroes as Hercules or our own King Arthur, he has twelve tasks to perform, each linked with one of the signs of the Zodiac. Dancing around the circle he shows off, in the person of the local hero, or a lad chosen by lot to play the part. He is armed with the Spear of the Sun and the Arrows of Passion, and when he has played his part, wooed the Goddess and, with her permission, bedded her, he fires arrows into the setting sun and departs on his great journey. This is Lady Day, when the Angel Gabriel came to Mary, Goddess in her own right, announcing her pregnancy, for it is nine moons to Yule.

When the white blossoms of hawthorn foam along the lanes, the God as Hunter, Guardian of Animals, Horned One, seeks his love in the forest, where she, Goddess of Change, is now hiding as a white doe. When he finds her he brings her to the forest clearing, and in the company of the whole community, leaps over the bonfire, wedding in the gypsy way.

The cycle continues; the pregnant Goddess ripens as the corn in the fields swells in the ear. Now the God is the Corn King, swathed in scarlet poppies, symbols so often of sacrifice, and blood upon the fields. Now, as the harvesters sweep across the golden land cutting swathes through the standing grain, the Corn King is ready to lay down his life for the benefit of the people. Garlanded in cornflowers blue as death, poppies red as blood, and corncockle golden as the setting sun, he who at this festival stands in for the God is cast down and laid on a bier or into a shallow grave in the field. Now his widow/mother mourns over his still form. She knows that the seed he sowed in her lives on, to be the new God in the dark of the year, but now she is all alone. In the North, Wakes Week, in Early August at Lammastide or *Lughnassadh*, recalls this traditional mourning for the sacrificed God. His spirit lives on and is preserved in the Corn Dollies, woven into traditional patterns, and samples of these are found in ancient Egypt, in Greece and all over the grain-growing lands.

Now the other fruits are gathered in, day and night are equal again, but darkness is winning, and the sun is fading in the sky. It is a time of reflection, gathering in those completed projects, sorting the good from the outworn, choosing the seeds for the new year's planting, be it crops for the land, ideas for the mind or inspirations of the heart. The flowers fade, but harvests are gathered of magical hazel nuts, instillers of wisdom when they feed the sacred salmon in his mysterious pool. Fungi are collected, for food and healing, and invoking dreams and visions in those whose sight was awakened by long training. St Michael, whose festival is on 29th September, is another Christianised form of the Sun God, and many of his churches are on high, pagan hill-tops. He balances the Dark Force, especially now, just after the Autumn Equinox, as summer balances winter, neither overcoming the other, in an eternal interchanging dance.

The Celtic Year draws to an end at *Samhain*, 'Summer's End', time of the Great Gathering, when all come home. It is a time of celebration and of remembering those who have parted from their earthly forms. The ghosts that enter the open doors and manifest in the sacred bonfire's smoke are kindly ones, old friends, grandparents, kindred from many ages, all thronging round with their wisdom, their accrued knowledge of the community and its needs. Now is the time of oracles, to see what will happen in the year to come. It is a time to bid farewell to those who have died, and welcome the new babies, and even the spirits of children scarcely conceived, or as yet unborn. All the Family come in and share the feasting, of the best and fattest of the beasts, the whitest bread, the sweetest honey and the lushest fruits at this short season of plenty, before the cruel winter's dearth.

Here the Goddess is both pregnant and the Old One, the Wise Hag, in this dark time when the Veil between the Worlds is thinnest, and knowledge and spiritual powers of magic can pass back and forth. She is always a changeable deity, paradoxical in her appearance, able to shape-shift in human and animal form, yet always being herself, in whichever guise best suits her purpose. She is the Ruler of the Otherworld, wherein her God/Lover rests, between his evolving incarnations. She is Persephone, Queen of the Dead and the Unborn, Bringer through the Veil of Life those to be born, carrying across the dark, still waters of the River of Night those who have passed from the world of flesh. She is All-Knowing, All-Seeing and All-Revealing to those who dare to ask her the right questions.

Like the Mystery Plays, based on the stories of the Old Testament, the story of the Goddess and her Son/Lover/

Sacrificed God was acted out by members of the community, in fields or barns, in small cottages and the squire's hall, as mimed or mumming plays, some of which endure. Parts were cast by drawing a lot, or finding a bean in a cake, so that the Old Ones made their own choices for their changing forms. Without set words, each actor was allowed to be inspired directly from the Goddess/God they were playing. Actions, songs, music, mime or words told each year a new version of the eternal story. Little of this was recorded in writing, but it is written on the waters, patterned in the branches of trees, and sung by the birds in the dawn chorus.

If you decide to set out upon the Old Road you will come to understand something of the simplicity of the traditional festivals for, whoever you are, you will discover the deities within you. They are your magical ancestors, their feasts are part of your own unfolding pattern. In winter you may rest, reviewing your last cycle of work and achievement, failure and loss. In you will sleep the child of your evolving self, born in the darkest night at Yule – soul-son of the Sun of Life. Cleansed and refreshed, when the first flowers show in your garden, go forth, Goddess renewed, or as her Champion, initiated into the New Year. Set forth your own list of the Twelve Tasks to be performed from March to March. Seek out your partner; within, as the secret other half of your own being, true Soul-Mate, or examine your relationships with those around you. How does your beloved benefit from your relationship?

By midsummer you should have a greater understanding of what you are going to achieve, and the 'crops' that you have sown, at home or at work, in dreams or in creativity will be flourishing in whichever field of life they are planted. As Lammas arrives, old Saxon Loaf-mass when the new flour was ground, you might be able to take a breather. Look at your opposite God/Goddess within. How has that Great Being strengthened you, brought you light or courage, love or understanding? What will you be able to lay before the altar of offering when the harvest is examined in the autumn days?

As winter approaches you will need to look within. What part of you has died, or been cast off? What part of you has an understanding of the Otherworld, gained through regular meditation or long, quiet chats with the God or Goddess in Nature? Learn to listen, to be still and hear with that inner ear the voices of the Old Ones. Watch your dreams for wisdom, and your intuition for awoken senses. Begin a new year with a new vision, realistically aimed at what you can achieve. Feel the ebbs and flows of the yearly tides, which bring forth and which sweep away certain aspects of your life, and learn to flow with them.

Exercises

After two moons of considering the Old Ways you ought to be seeing changes in your world view and your attitudes to things. If you have been able to spend a few minutes every day thinking about or meditating on the pagan gods or the old feasts, or the meaning of the religious life, you may be discovering new depths to your character.

Here are a few more matters to consider during the third moon.

Look at ancient sacred sites, on the ground if you can, or in books, and consider what mighty motives encouraged the ancient peoples to construct such enormous circles of stones, causeways or hillforts. How much effort, time and meditation are you willing to give over to your own rediscovery of the Old Ways and making contact with the First Parents? Are you actually doing anything, researching into local customs, building up lists of God and Goddess attributes, the kinds of trees in your area? Or are you still just thinking about it?

Consider the times of the old feasts, add these to your Calendar Circle, as well as the Green and White Harvests of each. What colour is the Harvest of Twelfth Night, do you imagine? Why do you think most modern witches ignore this date? Decide what symbols, like an Easter egg, you could have on open display in your home for each of the festivals, and draw these into your Calendar Circle.

What did Rites of Passage celebrate? Have you gone through any? What do you think the pagan ones are, and when would they happen? How do mumming plays fit into the ongoing record of the Old Ones?

Go out and look at the moon, watch her face among the clouds and see how you feel. Draw her light into your awareness and feel it waking up your psychic powers. See how the patterns of your dreams reflect the phases of the moon. Record what you find in your Book.

Discover some seasonal songs, folk tales or local myths.

Where do you think you could make friends who have interests in folklore, the Old Ways or pagan religion? Have you tried to get in touch with other people? You could leave messages in library books as bookmarks so that other readers of the same subjects could contact you. At least such folk would be nearby and perhaps on the same quest.

Here are some more books to sample:

Sir James Frazer, *The Golden Bough* (Century)
Vivianne Crowley, *Wicca; The Old Religion in the New Age* (Aquarian)
Dr Anne Ross, *Life and Death of a Druid Prince* (Century)
Joseph Campbell, *Hero With A Thousand Faces* (Princeton University Press)
George Ewart Evans, *The Horse, Power and Magic* (Faber)

4.

A CIRCLE BETWEEN THE WORLDS

Wind comes from the spring star in the East;
Fire from the summer star in the South;
Water from the autumn star in the West;
Wisdom, silence and death from the star in the North.

> Fiona Macleod: *The Divine Adventure*

A circle is perhaps the oldest pattern set out by people, recognised by artists, acknowledged by tiny children. It is a symbol of eternity, of equality, of permanence and of change. The face of the rising sun is round, the repeating plosh as raindrops splash into puddles forms recurring circles, the patch of light born of a single flame or a mighty bonfire sheds warmth and illumination in a circle. From huddles of playing children to the greatest gatherings of learned people, the shape they make is often a circle, where all can be heard, all can offer advice, all can equally participate in whatever is being arranged. So it is with magic.

The circle cast by the ceremonial magician or swept by the old wise woman's broom on her earthy floor represents a kind of spaceship, a time traveller's craft whose occupants may be transported to other times or other places. Its use is ancient, its power is unfailing. It can be protective, calming, healing, invigorating. It may be as small as the span of your arms or stretch, like the great Earth Zodiacs, across many miles of countryside. It may be created by your will to bring you inner peace for a few moments of meditation, or built of mighty stones and earthen banks over hundreds of years, enduring for thousands, as at Avebury, Callanish or Stonehenge.

Students have asked me if it is always necessary to have a magical circle set up in order to perform any kind of magical work, and like so much of the Old Arts, the answer is a paradox, being 'yes and no!' The greatest skill every witch, magician, druid or healer needs to develop is that of intuition. Literally 'inner teaching', it is that sense of 'rightness' about any action, thought or esoteric activity. When you have had some practical experience in the magical arts you will know, intuitively, if this is the moment to cast a circle or not. Only you can know that for yourself, no book can tell you, no teacher or school of thought can dictate it. You have to decide this minor point, as with many others as you go through your training in the coming years.

Mentally and physically, setting up a magical circle will probably be the first ritual act you will need to attempt. It can be a very simple procedure, taking a moment or two of thought, a few minutes of action. In other circumstances, or in the company of friends or companions on the path, it might take half an hour or even longer. It will be for you to experiment, explore your likes and dislikes, your personal situation and the location of your working. To begin with, it really is worth the bother of doing this small ritual carefully and completely; as you become more experienced the process may be shortened, simplified or even internalised, so that it is done in your head, instead of inside your house or garden or favourite wooded grove.

Like other paradoxical matters in magic, ritual circles are square! Acknowledgement is always given to the four points of the compass, 'the Quarters', perhaps by offering a symbol of the Elements commonly associated with each, or by the welcoming of a protective being, archangel, totem animal or elemental force. There may be a setting out of a sacred object, the lighting of a candle or the invocation of a goddess or god name to help with the ritual. One group of modern witches uses the names of the four winds, and though the names they use are the Greek ones, the old folk of Britain sometimes called upon, 'A pale wind and a purple wind, a black wind and a white...' to sweep away interference from their sacred place, protect it from harm and empower their spells.

The first consideration is space. If you are working indoors you will be limited both in the amount of room you have to make sacred, and how wild your activities within that space may be, because dancing, singing, waving a wand or even lying full length to receive divine inspiration are all possible aspects of the work. It does rather sadden me that some modern witches are keen to be sky-clad (naked) and free, but as a consequence take off their clothes and have to wear a house! Surely it is better in the eyes of the Earth Mother to wear comfortable clothes but be out of doors, in the wind and moonlight? A light robe, a warm cloak or even a special coat kept just for such encounters with Nature will not stop the channelling of power which can move the stars in their courses. Out there, the voices of the wild can answer your summons, give reply to your request or, as omens, fulfil your prayers.

Again, you will have to choose, but if you are new to these arts it may be easier and feel safer to be indoors, in familiar surroundings, where you can find items to use for the marking out of the square circle. The simplest set of symbols of the Elements of Earth, Water, Fire and Air are earth from the garden, water from the tap, a lighted candle and something scented. You can use a rock, pebble or slab of wood, which grows in the ground, for Earth. You may, if you are going to drink it, use spring water, fruit juice or wine for Water. Fire really does have to be something alight, although a smouldering joss stick could be used to represent both Fire and Air. For Air you could use some kind of incense, burned on proper charcoal, or a sweetly scented flower, pot-pourri, even a fan or a feather. Out of doors in a natural place, you may be surprised at what you can easily discover to represent the Elements – from tiny acorn cups of Water, to aromatic shrubs for Air, a red or yellow flower or leaf for Fire, and any kind of soil, stone, wood or sand for Earth.

These traditional four Elements represent the spokes of a wheel, which give it both balance and power. By calling upon these traditional Elements you create a kind of vortex which spins the energy you are drawing up from the Earth herself and mixes it with the power that is flowing down from the sky, making a potent source of magical force by which your spells will be made to work. You cause this power to move because in your ritual or in your mind you will be walking, dancing or sweeping around the circle, like a spoon in a teacup, stirring these balanced lines of energy into a cord of light which, rather like a twisted electric cable, can direct the energy where it is needed. As your psychic vision improves you will actually be able to see the Elemental power as different colours, or as flows of rainbow light, or sense them as heat or coolness.

You will need to write little poems or invocations to welcome or recognise these forces. 'Earth beneath and Sky above, Bless me ever with your love. Power of Nature, strength of Earth, Help me to find my own true worth. Flow of Water, rain in spring, Grant my heart the joy to sing. Fire of summer, light of flame, Guide me to my lifelong aim. Wind of autumn, breath of Air, show me peace beyond compare. Circle round and Light within, Guard me now, your human kin.' As you say each of these short invocations (or ones you have made up which are better poetry or more appropriate to your own symbolism) face up for Sky, look down for Earth, point to North for Elemental Earth, West for Water, South for Fire, East for Air. (You will either need to recognise where the points of the compass are from seeing stars or the sun in the sky, or buy yourself a reliable magnetic compass from a hiking or Scout shop.)

Ideally you will need to walk around the circle to each of these points in turn. If you do it just like that you will find you are going anti-clockwise, or widdershins as they say in Scotland. Now many modern witches do not like the idea of going anti-clockwise, not realising that that is the actual direction the Earth herself turns, so it is up to you. At the beginning of your work you may well be clearing things away, be it furniture or old ideas. Anyway, to get over this problem you can form a vortex clockwise by walking from North round three-quarters of a circle until you get to the West, where Water should be. Say the words, then do three-quarters of a clockwise circle to Fire in the South, and finally three-quarters of a circle to East where the symbol of Air will be. Face the centre and imagine a great circle of white-gold light sweeping round you and at the very centre, inside your own heart, a tiny diamond-bright point of silver fire.

Just try this very basic exercise, when you have cleared a physical space and cleaned it as well as you can. Place the four symbols of the Elements in their respective places; learn which is in which direction so that you will be able to look West from North, or South from East and so on without hesitation. Learn also to turn to your right for clockwise (deosil) or to your left for anti-clockwise (widdershins). When you have set out the Elements and walked the three whole circles it takes to do as above (or the single circle if you don't mind going widdershins), sit in the centre, relax and close your eyes. Feel the circle around you, as if it were a circular magical carpet which is tilting and building up energy, ready to lift you off and take you to the Place of Witchdom, the Old Land, where the Goddess and her Love are ready to meet you.

Be physically still, absolutely silent, and just sense, listen and become more aware than usual. After just a few minutes, get up and unwind the circle, the opposite way to how you began. In your own words thank each Element and bid them farewell. You cannot command these powers to visit you, nor should you try to banish them. They are parts of the balanced universe and it is your awareness of them that is being awakened, not their physical presence, because they are everywhere all the time. Always be polite and respectful, for it is a higher aspect of your own being you are really talking to at this stage. The more slowly and gently you practise these simple first steps, the more powerful they may become. Always take care, clear up, put things away, and really make an effort to feel the difference in the space you have temporarily made sacred.

In earlier times it was not necessary to sanctify an area for magic for among the natural places the world over there are extra special spots. High hills or mountain tops where the Sky Gods rest on their journeys; by springs and wells where the Goddess of the Inner meets the Goddess of the Outer Earth; in caves, wombs of the Earth Mother, and in sunlit glades in the Wildwood, where Jack-in-the-Green greets his children, human and animal alike. Some of these places had their power delineated by the construction of banks of earth, or waterways, or upright rings of stone, or even a single standing stone. Some were recognised as holy because of a special tree that grew there, or a strange rock not common the landscape, or because a poet had a dream there, or someone was healed or received a vision of the future. These things can still happen if we are willing to give them credence, and seek out the places where they might occur.

Specially powerful are the Markers of Memory, quiet spots often under the spreading arms of hawthorn or beech, the trees of the Goddess of Spring, and of the Book. (In earlier times writing was carved onto boards of beech wood.) In a dreamlike state it is possible to hear again the timeless stories, the hero tales, the poems and verses which record the ancient wisdom, written on the breeze; of the hymns to the Goddess, sung in her own sacred voice, unheard in the clatter of the modern world. It was to such places that the harpers, bards and storytellers of old would resort, to gain inspiration or hear, coming through the gates from some Otherworld, the music of another sphere.

You will gradually come to recognise such places, many of them unregarded yet close to the habitations of ordinary people, accessible in the everyday world, once you know what to look for. You will also discover such sacred spots are almost invisible to ordinary people, too, and that by being there in the right frame of mind, you are protected and unseen. Those who perform their magic in such places are seldom disturbed by other people, nor is the work done there interfered with by the presence of children or animals nearby. These places are genuinely guarded, and it is up to you to learn to trust the Old Ones to defend your meditations or cloak your activities from the casual observer.

Much has been written about the need for swords and knives and cups and pentacles, but these are not all really necessary, especially to the solo witch or lone practitioner. What you might need can include a cup to drink from, made of pottery, wood, stone or horn, for such things are traditional; a really sharp knife to cut hazel dowsing rods, and a long walking stick or wand. Today the Swiss Army type knives are especially good, as they also contain corkscrews, awls for boring holes in wood or leather, and a file or even a small saw for rather thicker branches. There is often also a screwdriver, essential for changing the plug on the ritual ghetto-blaster, or rewiring the sanctuary lamp! The blades should be kept clean, if you ever cut food or herbs, and sharp! There is no place in modern magic for blunt blades, either symbolically or practically. Knives should cut, with the least damage to the tree or other material, and the least damage to the owner – more people are cut by blunt blades because far more pressure is used in making the cut, so the point slips jaggedly into your hand! A cut from a sharp blade will heal quickly and more cleanly too, if you have an accident. There is also the symbolic aspect of using knives, often called *athames*, for magical work. This might have been relevant in medieval times, but today it is old hat. The same applies to swords. These are expensive, awkward or dangerous to carry about, and their symbolism can easily be represented by something far less threatening.

A long, forked walking stick, sometimes referred to as a 'stang', is both practical and useful. Such staffs have always been associated with wizards, and they were often carried for protection or to help with journeys on foot. In some pagan cultures they form the only altar, by being stuck into the ground at an appropriate place, and then being decorated with seasonal flowers or greenery, woven into a garland or twined up the staff. With the addition of a candle or lamp in a jar at the foot you have all you need to welcome any of the Old Ones. You soon learn to find twining stems of ivy, or woven grasses, or fronds of honeysuckle which can quickly be plaited into a circle and stuck on the forks of the staff, and into that base garland flowers, buds, leaves and berries taken from the trees, sacred at any season, can be woven. At the end of the ritual the garland may be hung on a tree branch so that birds or animals may eat the seeds or berries, or you can scatter the leaves back into the earth.

Traditionally the sacred direction moves around the circle as the year passes, and the time at which celebrations are held varies through the day and night. Standing at midnight at Yule or Christmas, face North, seeking out the Star of Hope which guides the Child of Promise back to Earth. Deck your staff with holly and ivy, and twine it with ribbons as red as life. At Twelfth Night, before dawn, turn just a little to your right, to face North-east by North, if you have a compass with all the divisions. Set a star at the top of the staff, twine golden ribbons, pine and other evergreen fronds about it (be careful if you use yew as the leaves are poisonous) and welcome the Three Wise Ones bringing gifts to you. At Candlemas, at first light, pick just a few snowdrops, early violets, and again ivy, symbol of the Spring Goddess, and place the staff to the North-east of the sacred circle. At the Spring Equinox or Easter bind a few yellow daffodils, sprays of jasmine and early white blossoms of the blackthorn in a wreath and place the staff to the East at the moment of sunrise.

When the hawthorn is in bloom, welcome the May Queen with a garland of her flowers, and the wild blossoms from every hedge and meadow. It was taboo to take may blossoms indoors, for the Goddess prefers to be greeted in the green world, not in a house. Dance round her South-eastern symbol in the morning. At noon on Midsummer's Day, garland your staff with St John's Wort with its golden sunray flowers, and all the brightest and best of the wild profusion in pinks and blues, mauves and whites, and the fresh green leaves from all the summer trees, especially oak. Face South and welcome the power of the Sun at his height.

When Lammas-tide brings in the corn and the Harvest God
dies in the field, dress the staff with red poppies, ears of wheat
or barley or oats, flowers from the hedges, trails of dog's
mercury, goosegrass and bindweed, and look to the South-west
where his flaming sun begins to descend in the afternoon. When
the harvest of the fields is in, seek out the wild fruits, berries,
seeds, and trailing old man's beard to twine around your staff,
at sunset, facing West. Lay nuts and apples at the foot of the
pole as an offering to the wild things of nature and scatter
crumbs and seeds.

In the dark evening of Hallowe'en deck the staff with
periwinkles, flowers of death so often used to garland those who
went to the scaffold, with branches of yew, and bright rowan
berries, hips and haws, and the black fruits of sloes and elder if any
yet remain. Look out through the open door to the North-west,
watching for the visit of those who have travelled into otherworlds,
through death, beyond birth, or those First Ancestors, our shared
kindred, Old ones, Great Ones, Parents of All.

So the circle of the year is completed. Within a house it is not
so easy to sense the power which comes from each direction,
and if you wish to hold elaborate rituals at each of the Old
Feasts, do try to spend just a few moments in the garden, or out
of doors, looking at the sun or stars, gathering with your own
hands the flowers or greenery. Please don't just buy cut flowers,
they are so forced and artificially fed. Even a few flowering
weeds have more life. If you don't like cut flowers at all, why
not plant a few suitable herbs, flowering plants or small trees in
pots so that each can form the centrepiece of your celebration?
Stood at the foot of the staff, itself set in a heavy base like a
bucket of sand, and decorated with coloured ribbons chosen to
suit the season, the flowers and leaves are so much more
evocative than a box altar.

This really works best of all out of doors, even in somewhere
as tame as your back garden. If you think you might be
overlooked, just consider how often in the last six months you
have noticed what your neighbours were doing. If you have
never noticed them, I doubt if they would notice you. If you
mentally make your circle one of invisibility then you will not
be seen, as I have proved over the last 25 years. Being able to
celebrate rituals or festivals in both private and public places, at
dawn, noon or at night, I have never been interrupted, and
when I have been in the company of others, we have not been

disturbed, even if other people happen to be in the same area. Learn to trust the Great Ones, in whose honour you are meeting, and whose help you are seeking, and they will surely assist in your guardianship.

Another kind of circle you will need to become aware of is the great circle of the turning year and the four mighty tides which sweep through our lives, whether we are aware of them or not. These have been described by followers of High Magic as the Cleansing Tide, between Yule and the Spring Equinox, the Growing Tide from March to June, the Reaping Tide from Midsummer to the Autumnal Equinox, and the Resting Tide from September to Yule again. Broadly they follow the pattern of the agricultural year, but they work on both the inner psychic levels of the initiate or novice, and on his or her magical work. It is often felt that the dark winter months immediately after the bright lights of Christmas are dull and dispiriting. It is a time of changes, often seemingly for the worst, when friendships falter and depression can set in. Scientists are now saying that a lack of Vitamin D caused by the diminution of natural sunlight at this time can affect people, but those who are wise see that there is a much more ancient reason than that. It was always a hard time; old folk might die, babies fail to thrive when food was scarce, and indeed, sunlight and vitamins available in fresh food would have been in short supply, but there is an inner current that flows through our lives, too.

Certainly the death rate in Britain does increase in January and February, and hearing of deaths through illness or poor conditions does not help if you are feeling 'under the weather' already. However, as it is the Cleansing Tide it is really time to take affairs into your own hands and be prepared to discard all those unsatisfactory relationships, those cluttered cupboards of the psyche full of unfinished work, those half-completed projects from a few years ago. Be brave and firm and throw them out, recycling whatever can be saved. Things *will* end at this time, unbidden, but the more that you are able to recognise the unstoppable power of this Tide the more you can use it instead of allowing it to simply wash through your life like the February floods flowing through the land. Be prepared for change, which, after the inevitable upheavals, will prove to be for the best, just as the newly cleaned house rewards you for the work required to make it spotless.

The Growing Tide brings expansion to all your magical plans, after they have been weeded and cleansed by the previous months of dissolution. New ideas should blossom, you should discover companionship, shared activities, and an outgoing sense of progress and success. This will run through March, April and May, right up to Midsummer, when again the great tides of the cosmos change.

The Midsummer Solstice brings the start of the Reaping or Harvesting Tide when those plans, skills, abilities and new directions which have flourished begin to pay off for the hard work required to make them successful. New talents will show their worth, whether it is the understanding of the Tarot cards, or a method of healing, or simply that your relationship with the Old Ones begins to pay dividends, and you gain self-confidence and support from these eternal sources of power and wisdom. Not only will you be able to benefit from these new-found abilities, but by using them as extra sources of information you will see more clearly the life-path that lies before you. You will begin, quite literally, to reap the benefits of all your early efforts each year.

When that harvest is gathered in and Nature goes to rest, so your own pattern will enter a much more peaceful and reflective time. You will be able to assess your personal progress, and be more willing to allow the subtle inner skills and awarenesses to come to the surface. Although this may seem to be a fairly gentle Tide, it is both positive, like the Growing Tide, and powerful. When you have gathered your wits at summer's end, you will be able to acknowledge your triumphs, and failings, which will be safely cast away in the following Cleansing Tide, so the cycle will continue. Both success and failure are natural parts of the system of individual progress, within the Old Arts, whether those of the solo witch or of the ceremonial magician. You will gradually be testing your own powers, sometimes succeeding, and occasionally over-reaching yourself and making mistakes, from which you will learn valuable lessons.

Gradually you will discover how cyclic the nature of many parts of life really is. Relationships may follow similar paths, of development, stability and decline, just as the trees show little life, full summer green, and a gentle decay into rest. Similarly the stories of the Goddess and her Consort show how she changes, grows, develops and seems to fade away, as the bright moon in the clear sky. You will understand that all life is concerned with change, and that both an upsurge of power and a slow descent into decay are natural and right. We cannot continue to surge forward without occasionally withdrawing, resting and casting away those things, ideas, relationships and experiences which are outworn or outgrown. To many people, such a recognition requires considerable courage, for casting away anything may seem an intolerable action, just as failing at anything is a great heartbreak. Yet it is being willing to dare, to reach further, think deeper, and travel beyond the limits of ordinary life, in the inner worlds of psychism and magic which makes following the Old Ways so fascinating.

Eventually you will learn that the circles which form so

important an aspect of Green Magic are actually spirals, turning about a still centre, yet actually rising through different planes of existence. Within this magical cone of power you will discover all the talents you have for making magic, for healing, for divination, and here, in the quiet circle you will eventually come to meet the Goddess of the Land and her Lord of Life.

Another circle which may become important to you is that of friendship. The Old Arts are not for the self-centred, the selfish or the power-hungry. They are not learned by the very young, the cruel or those who seek sexual gratification or domination over others. The Old Arts have a very high ethical foundation. The main object of entering any magical circle, pagan or High Magic, is to improve yourself, to grow in wisdom, to serve others through your growing skills. The newspapers are all too ready to suggest that witches harm children or sacrifice animals, commit perverted sex acts or use drugs. All these have *no* part in the Craft, the Old Religion or ceremonial magic. Many witches live in close-knit families, keep pets, are vegetarian or even vegan. Most seek out a loving and long-term partnership, nearly always within marriage, although in some cases a civil ceremony has been replaced with a pagan handfasting when, in the presence of the Goddess, the couple make vows of love to each other.

None of the reputable covens or training schools will consider very young people, below about eighteen years, unless they are part of a pagan family, when some training might be given. Those who offer initiation would not expect young folk to be ready, mentally, spiritually or religiously, until they were at least 20; often it is older than that. Certainly there is no upper limit, and some very mature and even retired people have discovered the Old Ways and seen then that they provide a spiritual path hitherto missing in their long lives. Within the Work there are many close friendships, working partnerships where absolute love and trust form a strong foundation to the relationship. Some of these are life-long bonds, and others last only while a particular piece of work, or healing or training is taking place.

The best way that any would-be or practising witch can serve the community is by being a valuable member of that society. It is often the case that a neighbour has been involved with magic or the Old Path for many years, but you only know of their good works because they are always cheerful, with an optimistic comment on the weather or the world situation. If you are in need they will help. Only later on might they let slip that they are interested in country traditions, alternative healing methods, folklore or some such thing. Real witches do not, and never have, called themselves 'witches'; that is a term applied by others. They might say they are interested in the Old Ways, even that they see themselves as pagans, but though all witches are pagans of one sort or another, not all pagans are witches. Some are members of orthodox faiths as well.

If you begin to set out your circle, become aware of its protection, its stillness, and the opening up of your own abilities which happens whilst you are within it, you will learn a valuable lesson; no one can learn for you. Remember, too, that if you go in for banishing rites, copied out of some other book, you might find yourself banishing friends, lovers, pets and many of the good things in your life. If you have to set up a guarded space for your meditation, then remember to take it down at the end. At the start, you may not be able to sense or see such circles, but they are there, real and effective right from the very beginning, so make sure all are gently swept away, and any Great Powers which you have invited to help you are duly thanked, to be welcomed again on another occasion.

Exercises

After spending several months mainly thinking and researching and developing your curiosity as to the origins of things which happen around you all the time, it is time to start the most basic practical exercises.

If you have been part of a magical group or coven some of the ideas may seem very simple or even primitive, compared to the lengthy speeches, 'Goddess Charges' and complex rituals of coven witches. Well, they are. Magic in any form is essentially simple, because most of it is made to work within your consciousness, and is seen in 'the mind's eye'. All the drama, ritual gestures, paraphernalia, witch tools and statues are unnecessary to making magic work. They only help set the psychological scene within the mind of the practitioner, who has to make an individual, genuine and sincere contact with the Great Ones in whichever guise he or she seeks to meet them, and then the power will flow. Think about it. Magic is extremely ancient and its power is undiminished by the ages. In the earliest times people did not have all the clutter of civilisation, and much of it becomes unnecessary props once the direct link is made. Here are a few of the most effective and basic considerations.

Go into the countryside with a sharp saw or knife and find a single branch of either an ash or hazel bush which you can cut to make a staff about as tall as your shoulder. Ideally it should be fairly straight and have a fork at the top. (Yes, certain suppliers do offer these for sale at a price, but you are supposed to be learning the Old Arts for yourself. Save your money and make the *effort*!) Carefully trim off side branches and, if you can, offer something to the tree, even if it is only spit. (Some water and plant food would be good.) Take the staff home, smooth the rough bits and allow it to dry, hung up to keep it straight. Round the tips and if you are clever, carve it, or decorate it in some other way. You should leave the bark on. Learn to love and respect your staff for it is the altar, the centre of your working. Discover how to make garlands, either as circles which can hang from the fork, or be twined around the upright. If you sharpen the bottom it will be possible to stick it into the ground.

Start learning to make a magical space, as described in this chapter. Do it silently, in your garden, and then in wilder places. Create it with your will, feel its power and guardianship. Know it is real.

List under columns headed North, West, South and East the symbols, natural and magical (as on the Tarot suits), colours, times of day or seasons, sacred animals, scenery for inner journeys, and all the other things which you will discover as an ongoing exercise to be kept in your Book of Illumination.

Go for a walk in the country and find a natural object which will represent each Element; Earth, Water, Fire and Air. Make a circle with them at the Quarters.

Here is a selection of books to try this moon:

Doreen Valiente, *Natural Magic* (Hale)
John and Caitlín Matthews, *The Western Way Vol I* (Arkana)
Dolores Ashcroft Nowicki, *First Steps in Ritual* (Aquarian)
Marian Green, *Magic for the Aquarian Age* (Aquarian)

You might now be ready to design, if not make, a garment for magic, a simple tabard or robe (as described in several of the above books) or a kaftan from an ordinary pattern. (There are some good books of theatrical costume in most libraries, which give very simple designs which are ideal as they have minimal shaping or sewing!)

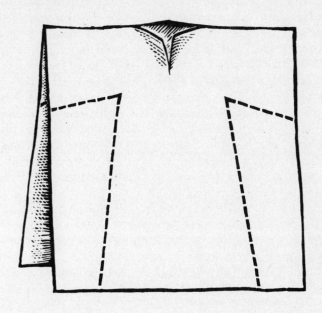

5.

THE JOURNEY TO THE OTHERWORLD

I returned across the water to my temple; that dangerous journey across running water which absorbs and carries away magnetism and may break up the projection. In my temple, from which the astral forms which we build with so much care are never banished, I laid my two hands on the altar and faced the Moon-symbol that hung upon the mirror that is a two-way door to another plane, and in the mirror I saw my own reflection with the image of the Great One behind me, and to that shadowy form, built up by the mind, I surrendered the vital force that I had drawn into myself . . .

Dion Fortune: *Moon Magic*

Magic is the art of causing changes in consciousness, for it is in an altered state of consciousness that the seeds of magic are sown, that the visions of past, future or distant events are seen, and when the true communions with the Great Ones in their many forms may take place. Many modern witches will not make the effort of learning to still their bodies and awaken their minds by meditation; or practise the arts of visualisation, that magical inner story-telling; or expand their powers of concentration through determination and regular work. These are all basically very simple activities, but because of their seeming ease, they are seldom credited, by newcomers, with the power they offer.

To be able to control the state of your own conscious awareness is a very valuable skill. It requires lots of regular and consistent practice to bring that most fractious part of our beings under control, and yet without it all magical acts, rituals or divinations are pale shadows of what they could be, if the will is there to direct the inner perceptions accurately towards the goal of the moment. This practice can be hard and seemingly unrewarding work, perhaps for days or even weeks, but suddenly that subtle control is gained when the physical body can be perfectly relaxed and at peace, and the mind is sharply focused and alert. It is in this poised state of resting wakefulness that the clarity of vision, the perceptions of symbols, the voices of the gods, and the clear apprehension of other realms of existence and the beings that dwell there are achieved. It can take a lot of effort, but nearly everyone who really wants to master the arts of magic can teach themselves these methods by making an attempt every day, until it happens.

Today we do not have many moments of quietness in the hustle and bustle of modern life, whereas our ancestors, living a much slower, simpler and more physically demanding lifestyle, travelled at the speed of the carthorse not the high tech horsepower of the car. Many tasks were performed by hand, laboriously, and whilst the body toiled at the plough, the loom, the pitface or the axe their minds were free to wander. In those unlettered days, memory was sharp, as was vision and awareness of the minutiae of wildlife, the changing face of Nature, the growth, ripening and decay of plants, the activities of animals and the interaction of their human kin. They would not call their inner musings 'meditation', but often practical solutions to everyday difficulties or improvements to the patterns of work would arrive at the threshold of awareness, just as 'realisations' arrive for a more modern meditator.

It is necessary to realise that the greatest asset to magical work, especially that performed as a lone practitioner, is the ability to enter an altered state of controlled consciousness, for it is this which allows the seeker to come face to face with the Old Ones in their own worlds. It is by mentally entering this altered state, within a magical 'flying' circle, that the Otherworld becomes visible, real and interactive with the traveller between the worlds. Once the circle has been set up it should become a vehicle to allow you to travel through time, space or the realms of Nature, where all things which change have their roots and primal patterns, and where changes which happen in our world can be initiated.

There is no simple way of learning how to venture swiftly into the Otherworld, except by regular experiments. No one else can do it for you, or really teach you. What you experience there will be personal, so the accounts of another person's adventures will not help you. The closest ordinary experience which you may have often had is that of total absorption in a good book, or perhaps a film. A book is really the nearest comparable activity, for then you are 'creating' the scene, the characters, the ambience, and if you are absolutely engrossed in the words the whole experience takes you outside time and your present space. What you will need to learn, for your magical experiments, is to be totally absorbed in the building up of the scenery, sensing, with your eyes closed, the atmosphere, the wind, the light of sun or moon. It requires both concentration and relaxation. If you tense your muscles, as you might do whilst trying to perform some feat of physical strength, you will be unable to transfer your awareness to the Otherworld. Like many other occult skills, it is a 'knack', an art which is learned all in one. You cannot half-meditate, or nearly ride a bicycle, or just about swim. In each case there is a state of not being able to, and then, albeit badly at first, the actual ability to meditate, swim or ride a bike. Again, practice makes perfect.

If you are already well able to immerse yourself in a good book and so forget the world, the time or the everyday activities around you, the inner arts will come easily to you. The method used in the West is the very ancient art of storytelling, familiar to many of us from childhood, familiar the world over from the childhood of mankind. The only difference between seeing storytelling as an entertainment or as a form of magical training and illumination is the effort the listener has to make. In the magical context, the listener tries to create, see or enter into the action of the story, meet the hero, walk through the forest, encounter the dragon or challenger, discover the treasure. Of course, today we have the Dungeons and Dragons type of game, both as books and as video games where, by making decisions as you follow the plot, you conquer enemies, gather weapons and treasure or seek out advantages. In the magical arts, which are probably as old as tribal sorcery, you may meet real characters, gods and goddesses, discover very real-seeming dungeons, become a hero or heroine on your own account. The more effort you are able to put in to perceiving what is being described, the more you can concentrate, in a relaxed way, on the action, the clearer and more real will your experience become.

Today, to help all those who are interested in the magical arts, there are many inner journeys, 'path workings' and creative visualisations on cassette tapes. I have made some basic ones myself. This is the most effective way of learning the technique because you can relax, sit comfortably in a quiet place and, using a tape player or personal stereo, simply listen to the words and build up the scenes as they are described. This is much easier than reading from a book, a section at a time, whilst also trying to remain relaxed and switched off, and of course, it is impossible to read with your eyes shut. Most people dislike the sound of their own voices on tape but while you are learning, it really is worth the effort of slowly reading the myths of the Goddess or a description of a place sacred to the Sun God on to a tape, and allowing yourself to build up the scenes in your mind's eye, rather than sacrificing the relaxed state to read from a book. You may find that a friend with a calm and gentle voice might be willing to read a suitable text from a book for you.

What ought to happen is that you enter a dreamy and pleasant state of mind, when your body is comfortably relaxed, and yet the images that you hear described unroll themselves before your inner vision. At any moment, if the phone rings or you hear the baby crying or something needs to be attended to, you only have to open your eyes to be back in the ordinary world. Of course, if you are sensible, you will cut off as many distractions as you can, for knowing that you might be disturbed is a sure way of making it impossible to relax properly. Over a few sessions, using the same narrative, you will find that the images become clearer, and that you start to sense the atmosphere, see the light of the sun, smell the greenery or the incense or whatever is being described. Like many similar sorts of activity, it does pay to hasten slowly. Take your time. One session each day for a week and then a few days off will produce far better results than three or four sessions in one day and then none for a month! The mind, like an animal, is trained most easily by techniques applied little and often. Regular attempts, first thing each morning or in the afternoon, are better than late at night or at irregular intervals.

Although this might seem a far cry from the activities of the old village witch or the tribal sorcerer, it is one aspect of a collection of arts which our forebears would have used more or less unconsciously. Our modern lives are permanently bombarded with sounds, music, pictures of other places, the activities of other people, whereas our ancestors had far less input, and their minds would have been freer to wander through time and space as they worked their way through the hard and boring grind of manual labour. We know from the vast hoard of folk songs and work songs that these hours each day were filled with new ideas, old tales and the rhythmic tunes accompanying each task. Of course, many of these songs were bawdy, but others recounted the most ancient legends, the history of the people or the job they were doing. There is a huge amount of sung and oral material largely ignored by modern scholars, yet it contains valuable insights into the depth of traditional wisdom, ancient lore, songs of worship and the seasonal feasts, if we can learn to value the simple things from the past.

Take a familiar folk song, like *Scarborough Fair*. It is a riddle song, about sowing seeds between the salt sea and the white strand, making a shirt without any seams and no needlework – parsley, sage, rosemary and thyme, all culinary and magical herbs. It is one of the challenge songs, old as the hills, in which the initiate seeks to win the hand of the girl he loves by performing some impossible tasks. These are similarly parts of many fairy stories where, because of kindly deeds towards animals, the heroine is helped to sort seeds, spin enormous amounts of thread or something similar. Underlying these is the Mystery, the magical heart of the myth wherein the main character is able to call upon Otherworldly help, often portrayed as small animals or birds, in order to perform some seemingly impossible task. Many of our modern pantomimes are based on such tales, like *Jack and the Beanstalk*, *Cinderella* and *Beauty and the Beast* where magical happenings are brought about. Many of these stories are very widely told, and often extremely old. Cinderella, for example, is found all over Europe, Africa and as far afield as China, in slightly varied local versions.

We need to become aware that there are many paths which lead to the Otherworld, many of them ordinary and well-known, but probably not recognised as having a magical application. Begin to look again at stories you read last as a child, or which you may be reading to your own children. See if they are still playing the old games, with ropes or rhymes or songs and actions. Even things like Hopscotch with its ten squares could be based on the magical Qabalistic Tree of Life, a diagram of the creation of the Universe, according to ancient Hebrew occultists! The story of King Arthur and his knights and their quest for the Holy Grail contains a vast amount of evolved material about the initiate's search for some hidden treasure, the tests of his common sense, his strengths, his religious beliefs and his relationships with young ladies. This particular set of legends contains many valuable clues about the ancient Celtic system of magic, seeing animals as guides or omens, seeking out wild places where hermits lived in sacred groves or dangerous Otherworldly beasts had their lairs. This ancient quest is still a valid part of our own heritage and, like the path of the solo witch, one which often had to be carried out alone, using individual skills and personal resources.

As you reread some of these traditional old tales and legendary cycles, see how what they are saying can be relevant to today's personal search for enlightenment and magical power. All the clues are there, but today we travel through the equally wild and frightening concrete jungle and our wildernesses are peopled with strangers or machines rather than giants and monsters. We still need to rescue the maiden from the dragon's dinner table but now may see she represents our inner female nature, or a part of the Goddess we can adopt during our rites of worship. We might understand that the faithful horse is our physical body, which needs to be properly fed, exercised and groomed, for without it we will not be able to travel through any worlds, let alone those inner realms wherein it can be safely left behind. We may need to sharpen the sword of our wits and strengthen the shield of common sense and good humour as we set off through the mindfields of the Otherworld, so that we are not frightened by anything we meet there, nor overawed by the power we shall discover. Both these things which may scare us on our magical journey and the upwelling of power initially come from within ourselves. We cannot banish them, or overcome them, anymore than we can cut off a foot or, on a sunny day, detach ourselves from our shadow.

The best and safest paths to the Otherworld begin in the wild places of this world. The image of a deserted moor, uncultivated meadows of wild flowers cropped only by deer and rabbits, sacred groves of small trees set about a sparkling spring, or a wild wood will each offer you a genuine and safe doorway to the Otherworld. So would a cave, or a sea-girt grotto, or an unclimbed mountain peak, but the first suggestions will be easier to imagine, clearer to see and are more gentle, as you make your first assays into the inner realms.

Here is a simple exercise. Read the words a few times to impress them into your memory and then take a comfortable, upright posture with your back supported by a chair or tree. Breathe deeply half a dozen times, slowly and gently, feeling all tensions leaving your body, yet remain awake and alert, though physically relaxed and at peace. Close your eyes without screwing them up, and feel around inside your body for any discomfort or tension, making sure that neither your arms nor your legs are crossed, so that your energy flow will not be impeded as you enter the Otherworldly state. Then, bit by bit, build up these images. As slowly as you need and as completely as you can, enter into each image in turn:

First, see a soft brown cloak of natural wool being wrapped around you. Feel its pleasant texture, its warmth and comfort. This will protect you, making you invisible if you are out of doors, or reduce your awareness of intruding thoughts or disturbances indoors. Become really aware of it before you go to the next image.

Now, still enclosed in the cloak of protection, rise to your feet and see that you are standing on a narrow path through a field of wild flowers. It is a pleasant sunny day with a light breeze touching your cheek. You may smell the scent of hay, the many flowers, and feel the wild wind blowing freely. You may hear the drowsy buzz of bumble bees, the chirrup of crickets, the hum of insects among the flowers, and the shush of the wind among the grasses. Otherwise it is very quiet.

You begin to walk along the path, seeing it wind along a hillside towards a small cluster of trees. You feel very peaceful as you stroll in the sunshine. Soon you draw near to the grove of trees, all deep green in the full leaf of summer. Perhaps you recognise young oaks, small ash trees, the darker green of holly, the feathery-edged leaves of hawthorn with clusters of green haws among them. You enter the cooler shade and begin to hear the chirping of birds, and the rustle of the light breeze in the branches. In the dimmer light you pause.

After a few moments, something brighter catches your eye and you walk on, winding among the trunks of the trees. You see the lush grasses beside the path dotted with white and mauve flowers. You begin to sense other presences, perhaps only birds or small animals, or perhaps those watching spirits which are found everywhere under Nature's care.

Carefully you make your way forward, for the trees crowd closer here, and the path has petered out amid the loamy brown leafmould that carpets the wood. You look around you, not sure which way to go.

You turn round, seeking the path, but it has vanished. The leafy

*branches seem to brush your hair, and the trunks of the trees feel as if
they are closing in. The dim green twilight darkens and you begin to feel
lost and alone. Before you there seems to be an arching doorway of
slender rowan trees, leaning in towards each other, and beyond them a
lighter glade seems to offer a safer path. You push your way through the
low branches, here and there scented with the peppery aroma from the
clustering white rowan flowers. It feels as if a door toward the light is
opening for you as you pass between the smooth, slender grey-green
trunks. Ahead there is a fallen tree, entwined with ivy and creepers, but
part of the bole is clear, and greatfully you sink down to sit and rest
awhile.*

*The light which seemed to fade under the trees now begins to brighten
and every leaf glistens and shimmers with dazzling points of sunlight.
The birds all sing in tuneless chorus. Around you the wind seems to
rustle the branches, and small whirlwinds raise twists of dust. As you
sense all these things at once, another great presence looms near to you,
and a bell-like voice speaks from behind you.*

*'Welcome, my child, why have you come through the Door in the
Heart of the Greenwood?'*

*You try to turn to see who is there, but your body is reluctant and all
you see is a greenish shadow out of the corner of your eye. Somehow you
manage to speak and answer. New questions follow, and you receive
answers for what may seem a long time.*

*Eventually there is silence, the light dims, the birdsong dies and the
trees are still. You look round and may just catch the departing swirl of
a green cloak vanishing between the tree trunks, a tall form moving
swiftly into the leafy gloom. For a few moments you ponder on what
has been said, and then slowly rise to your feet.*

*Looking between the arching rowans you see the path, now quite
clear and straight. You make your way along it. The trees that seemed
to press closely now lightly touch your hair, conferring a blessing. The
scent of greenery, wild flowers and soft loam fills your nostrils, and you
breathe deep of this free, fresh air. Soon you leave the wood, seeing how
tiny it appears, how safe and familiar the trees. You cross the flowering
meadow, again being acutely aware of the colours of the flowers, the
touch of the grasses, the twitter of rising skylarks and the low murmur
of bees.*

*As you look about you the scene grows misty and dim. You feel very
happy and relaxed, but those images, feelings and experiences linger
with you. Soon you are ready to open your eyes, and return gently yet
completely to your own familiar world. Return and remember!*

Perform this journey several times, always noting what you see, feel and hear – including distracting everyday noises, and the questions the Being in the Wood asked you. Each time you will discover new aspects of this very simple yet powerful exercise, for it is a key to the door to the Otherworld. When you become used to the technique, you will find that as you set out on this path, another may unfold between this world and the Otherworld. You will voyage on mental adventures of discovery, sensing new aspects of this inner realm. Its entry is free, its paths are protected, and anything you fear will have been brought with you.

Make some real journeys, too, to visit quiet country lanes, old villages, river banks, cliff-girt beaches and high, open moors. Here you will be able to discover that what you see in your inner vision, conjured in your own room or garden or quiet place, has genuine natural counterparts. Similarly, you will find that in the wild, the Great Beings of Nature, the gods and goddesses of the green world, the nature spirits, dryads or tree guardians, totem and real animals, mythical beasts, all may be encountered, if you go half way to meet them. That is a simple act of willing yourself into their presence, with a relaxed body, closed eyes and an awakened consciousness.

Only regular work at these basic exercises will ensure clear visions, full perceptions and valuable experiences. Both the real trips to the country and the practice runs in your own space need to work hand-in-hand, for both build up the data banks of knowledge, symbols and experiences.

Remember, you will be encountering real beings whose world interacts with ours, but to most people they are invisible and their touch is unfelt. Once you have walked in spirit through a few of the old doors to the Otherworld, you may begin to perceive ever more clearly where the two worlds overlap and interlock. It is for this reason that you cannot call up, command or banish any of the Old Ones you meet. They are always there and it is your own sight and ability to interact with them that you may command. Like muscles, the inner eyes of Otherworldly journeying need to be trained slowly, gently and carefully, to give the most rewarding results.

Every creature, tree, spring, wild stretch of countryside, Great God or nature spirit has its own place in the scheme of things. All may become visible to you, if you make the effort to get to know them. Be polite, respectful and reasonable in your dealings with these Old Ones from other dimensions. They can bring you wisdom, healing, power and love, and will ask little in return. Often they will give you gifts which, though they usually vanish inside you before you fully return to this world, are real and many are valuable in terms of the Otherworld. Always give thanks for such gifts, even if at the time of their receipt, you do not know what they are or what they may be used for. Each is probably a key to unlock entrances to your own doors of the Otherworld, behind which you may gain the knowledge, experiences, magical energy or divinatory skill which you most need.

One day you will start to see that there are doors to the Otherworld all round you, as there have always been. They may lead from your own street to fairyland, or from the city to the Heart of the Greenwood. You will come to understand, through personal experience, that inner sight is not the only way of apprehending these Otherworlds. Some you will only feel, sensing the ambience, the warmth, coolness or energy; others you will hear, speaking with many voices, inside your head or even heard with your ordinary ears. Some places or Beings from the Otherworld, especially animal forms to whom scent is a language, may be smelt or tasted on the air, in the way that the salty tang tells you that you are near the sea or that it is raining when the pungence of wet dog precedes the animal into the house. Our senses are blunted, even compared with our ancestors, by such bad habits as smoking, eating unnatural foods and living in centrally heated air, but we should use them to the full, especially when our sight, our predominant sense, is taken from us in the closing of the lids and refocusing on other realms.

You will soon encounter the magical paradox encompassed by the question, 'But am I making it all up?'. The whole matter hinges on the word 'make'. What you are saying (probably to yourself, as it is the sort of query which surfaces when you are struggling on alone) is, are you 'imagining' whatever you see, feel, smell or sense otherwise. The word 'imagine' and the word 'make' come from the same root! You are making yourself perceive in a new way, which perhaps at first seems irrational, but gradually you will find that the actual question has no meaning. It simply does not matter if you are making things up, or imagining them, or actually seeing and sensing things beyond your normal range, so long as you are actually learning to become aware of them. You can try to surprise yourself, in the way that some of the scenes you encounter in the Otherworld will surprise you. Then you will understand the nature of occult knowledge.

Elementals are natural energies associated with the elements of Earth, Water, Fire and Air. We can't really be sure what they are like in their own realms, for like all beings that appear to our clouded vision, they tend to be shaped by our own imagination. A simple example is an angel. Now, you can look at pictures throughout Christendom and see illustrations of robed figures with feathered wings, in various colours, designs and degrees of reality. Show such a picture to a foreigner or a child and they will probably be able to identify the image as that of an angel. Angels don't actually look like that – they are not flying people but great energy forms, shapeless and rainbow-hued, if you ever see them in their own forms, as you can if you ask them to appear like that. But human artists, over many hundreds of years, have created the stereotyped image, originating from some vision but interpreted into human form. The same applies to Elementals. They look like their element, flowing, streaming, illuminating, almost invisible giant vortices of power, but because they are willing to limit themselves to the stereotyped image constructed by humans, they may be perceived as nymphs or dryads or sylphs or gnomes. Once you learn to catch them unaware, by entering their worlds gently and without making cross-dimentional ripples, you may see them as they are. Do realise, though, that all these beings are huge, vast, lofty and expansive. Imagining them as little animal-like spirits diminishes them and demeans their might. They are eternal, awesome, potent and far wiser than we children of Earth.

Part of the Old Arts is the acceptance of other dimensions, other realms, alternate realities from which we are only cut off by ignorance, or perhaps over-keen scepticism. We cannot see TV pictures without a set, electricity and an aerial, but those waves of information are all round us. We cannot see Elementals or angels, but if we visualise them, so mentally providing the power, the aerial and the receiver, we may well perceive them. As we tune these senses, just as an engineer would tune a satellite dish, the picture becomes clearer, the sound more distinct and our understanding of what is being transmitted greater all the time. All of us are born with the ability to pick up these 'astral' signals from the starry heights. Many of us as children were well aware that we could travel through the air, meet fairies or animals or other childhood heroes. We encountered them most nights in our 'dreams' but now, as adults, we have to learn again that childlike simplicity, acceptance of what our adult logic tells us is improbable. That is the secret of walking into the Otherworld, realising that there can be things of which we are not aware in our everyday state of mind, but which the Old Arts may reveal to us if we trust intuition and our inherited wisdom. It may require us to make huge cultural leaps, but that is one aspect of 'becoming a witch' or walking the solo path towards the realms of the Great Ones. We will certainly be surprised, for that is a sure sign that something magical is at work in our lives, and that we have stepped through that filmiest veil of conscious acceptance, and so begun to see and experience for ourselves. Try it; it might genuinely change your life!

Exercises

Today we have psychological expressions to describe various states achieved during meditation and creative inner journeys. In the old days such states were part of the boring and repetitive work most people had to endure. Because mental distraction is a rare occurrence, those who use meditation as a vital tool for their inner studies have to learn this simple art, and surprisingly difficult it may prove to be.

The techniques which need to be worked upon during the fourth moon have to be mastered to make any magic work, and to allow the practitioner personal visions of the gods and goddesses on a controlled basis.

Start by reading a description of one of the deities and then, with your eyes closed and in a relaxed position, begin to retell that description to yourself, building up the image until it is clear. Try this for at least four days, for about fifteen minutes at a time.

Another valuable exercise is to look at a real flower or plant in front of you, then close your eyes and try to 'see' it in your mind's eye. You know it is real, it has life, but seeing it with your eyes closed may be very hard at first. Keep at it for as many sessions as it takes to get a clear impression of the plant. You can then mentally make it flower for a few sessions, putting forth buds, then blooms, then fruit or seeds. You will need to be able to create and then manipulate images as acts of magic, so the sooner you get the knack, the better.

Look at some familiar tales and see if you can discover the magical story within them. You may be surprised. How clearly do your favourite writers lead you into the world of their fictional works? Try to unravel the occult theme of any children's story you can get hold of, too.

Try out the inner journey as described in this chapter at least three times. Write down in your Book what you saw, felt, imagined and what changed between the first and third attempts. Write out your questions and the answers you received on each occasion.

Find time to walk in uncluttered places and build up an inner journey based on a real walk along a country lane, or by a river or the sea. Try also a couple of times and see what happens, comparing what you feel and sense with the deliberately magical journey into the Greenwood.

Why are the Beings of the Otherworld real? How can you prove this, if only to yourself?

Try to enter an inner place where you can meet the Elementals of Earth and then of Water. Write down what happened, then later, when you have had a lot more practise, try Fire and Air Elementals.

Is anything new happening in your dream life?

Here are some books with instructions about meditation or path working. (You might like to try some of the cassettes of inner journeys I have recorded – write to me care of the Publishers for latest details.)

Dolores Ashcroft-Nowicki, *Highways of the Mind* (Aquarian)
R J Stewart, *Magical Tales* (Aquarian)
Helene Hess, *The Zodiac Explorer's Guide* (Aquarian)
Naomi Humphrey, *Meditation: The Inner Way* (Aquarian)
Marian Green, *Experiments in Aquarian Magic* (Aquarian)

If you keep failing to enter the proper, relaxed frame of mind which makes these exercises produce results, realise you may be trying too hard, so play at it, make it much more of an experiment, gone about in an attitude of 'Well, it doesn't really matter, but let's give it a go!' Try also at different times of day; early mornings are usually best but midday, if circumstances permit, or early evening might work for you.

6.

SEEKING OUT PAGAN TRACES

The old pagan Britons were in the habit of having fairs when they assembled at their holy centres for the big sun festivals. The fairs went on just the same, whether they were pagan or Christian, and the missionary centres grew up where the crowds came together. When the king was converted they just changed the Sun for the Son. The common people never knew the difference. They went for the fun of the fair and took part in the ceremonies to bring good luck and make the fields fertile. How were they to know the difference between Good Friday and the spring ploughing festival?

Dion Fortune: *The Goatfoot God*

Although we are living in a Christian country many of the sacred sites, the dates of Church festivals, and celebrations in both town and country places have roots much older than those of Christianity. Today we may forget that the common folk, living in rural areas, had little to do with the state religion, and for much of its history, the rites they were made to attend were in Latin, so the unamplified prayers of the priests would have meant little to about ninety percent of the congregation. In their own way, and in places which were long sanctified by Nature herself, they conducted their own simple rituals. At the foot of ancient trees, outstanding rocks, hilltops, caves or fresh water springs were the traditional sites of offering, supplication and thanksgiving. These were the sacred places to those of the Old Religion. They needed no roof to cover their shrines save the starry night sky, or a canopy of green leafy branches. Their gods and goddesses were the First Beings, vast, ancient, endless and yet still approachable by the ordinary folk, with their everyday worries, woes and wishes.

Of course, many ancient sacred sites are well-known places of

historic and archaeological interest, famed for their vast circles
of standing stones, earthworks, banks, ditches, burial mounds
and barrows. The real antiquity of many of these enormous
projects of human endeavour is only now being fully realised,
and their age is being pushed back all the time. Many of the
really elaborate monuments, like New Grange in Ireland and
Stonehenge, may have been founded nearly 6,000 years ago,
and these have passed through many stages of construction and
reconstruction. These mighty monuments must have had
religious and magical associations and not merely been places of
ritual burial for a few chosen dead, any more than the vast
medieval cathedrals are simply extra special tombs for a few old
bishops!

As well as the huge and famous antiquities there are literally
thousands of much simpler, yet certainly as ancient
constructions all over Britain, Ireland, Europe and North
Africa, as well as around the Mediterranean Sea and on most of
its islands. Some timeless constructions are known to be
complex temples, probably dedicated to the Earth Mother in
whose shape they are constructed, for example on Malta and its
neighbouring island of Gozo, where many figurines of fat,
pregnant goddesses have been uncovered. In other places all we
now see are single standing stones, hummocks over sacred
mounds, or partial rings or rows of stones of various sizes. The
glory and power of some of these ancient sanctuaries has been
hidden, but those who are willing to use the old ways of seeing
may experience visions of these outdoor temples in their
heyday.

You can surprise yourself in this matter. Find a local place
with really ancient connections, be it tumulus, quoit, fogou or
hut circle, and try to visit it alone. Sit down, relax, and allow
your mind to cross the vast river of time which separates that
construction at its foundation from our modern, hurried world.
Sink into meditation, with a silent request on your lips and in
your heart to learn something of the wisdom which set up the
structure, the powers which were handled there, the aspects of
the goddess or god which were honoured. Become as still and
mentally alert as you can, and imagine a mist which wipes out
time building around you and the sacred place you are visiting.
Let the mist represent all the years that have passed and
gradually, as it fades away, you may well find that the
landscape you begin to see or sense is different. If there are

people about ask, mentally, that you can communicate with them, and that they recognise you are coming as a friend and seeker to their holy ground. What they may say to you will probably be heard in your head, or envisioned behind closed eyelids, but it should make sense to you.

Although this is a very simple exercise, if you have been practising some of the meditative arts suggested earlier you will have a sure road, and clear access to the knowledge of the past. Nothing is or can be entirely lost. We have simply forgotten the ancestral keys to what was once known, perhaps even by ourselves, in previous lives. We have also overlooked the powers of our ancestors too. No longer is the accrued wisdom of the grandparents passed on to their younger generations around the winter fireside, and the traditional skills of hand and mind shared in the garden or potting shed. Our grandparents may be dead, or shut away in an old peoples' home, or isolated by family splits or sheer distance. We do not reverence those people who are older, and may even have grown up mocking age and deploring old-fashioned ideas. Those who would walk in the ways of the Old Ones will have to relearn the links of kinship, the value of inherited knowledge and the power of forgotten lore.

Living in a world which is changing week by week instead of generation by generation, we may well not be able to keep up with the speed of change, and change itself is the very essence of magic. Magic is the art of working with change, predicting it and shaping it by our trained wills. The world is rushing by us at an ever-increasing pace, at this cuspal tide of Pisces going into Aquarius. Perhaps the hardest lesson we all need to learn is to slow down, return to the pace of the horse and cart, not the train or aircraft. By slowing down, we change our focus on the way we see things, just as in dreams we feel as if we are running through treacle or moving as if we were in the Moon's gravity rather than that of Earth.

By being still and watching Nature at work and play we refill our depleted stores of natural energy and our awareness of what the world is really about. We can watch people, animals, the flowers and trees around us, no matter how urban we New Age pagans may be, in exactly the same way that our real pagan ancestors watched their world pass the doorways of their little houses. It is by observation that we can judge the mood of people and animals. Scientists have given us the term 'body

language' with which wild animals and insects communicate
with each other, and humans unconsciously express some of
their innermost feelings, in a code few of us are trained to read.
An old country dweller could see a cow in a distant field and
know that she was ready to calve, or that a horse was going
lame, or that the household dog had scented a stranger, just by
the way each animal was standing. That sort of trivial
information was the vast store of knowledge on which the local
wise woman or cunning man thrived. Most of it was almost
intuitive; it was how the old dame, noted for her love spells,
would already know that the girl calling at her cottage for
guidance fancied a certain lad, or that one of the young fellows
had his eye on a particular married woman. She would know,
too, how best to fend off unsuitable matches or encourage, both
by magic and common-sense psychology, those couplings which
she approved of. Today we have computer dating!

Many of the old sacred sites, the ancient holy places and
healing springs are actually under our noses, but our television-
focused eyesight misses them out, because they don't come with
subtitles. We have to learn to look at anything which might give
us clues in a new light; reconsider the local customs, the
traditional dishes, the occasional fairs, or Morris dancers
outside the nearby pub. Each holds some of the tangled threads
with which we are bound to our magical and pagan heritage,
and given a little time, a bit of luck and some thought we may
well be able to untwist the skein and see again its sacred colours,
its secret pictures and its long-lost lore. For instance, every city
must have been founded near water. This may sound trivial,
but it is true! Somewhere, even under London (the
encampment of Llud, god-king before the Romans came), there
are healing springs, wells and old watercourses. Heard of
Sadlers' Wells theatre? Underneath is an ancient well, and it is
close to London Spa at Clerkenwell! Holborn, the 'holy
stream'; Fleet Street, with its underlying noxious Fleet Ditch;
the Strand – the watery connections are there if you start to look
for them.

Take many of the famous churches too – St. Paul's, built and
rebuilt many times but always on that hill, upon which in pagan
times there was a temple to the Moon Maiden, Diana. Perhaps
that was why the mystical Prince Charles elected to marry his
Diana there! Many of the city churches are linked by the
powerful 'ley lines' which equally join better known sacred

sites, like Glastonbury and Avebury. Temple Church near the River Thames, damaged in the last war, was set up by the Knights Templar, that magical brotherhood whose mysteries are another layer in the strata of the Western Mystery Tradition. Its remains still show the circular chapter house, surrounded by mysterious faces peering down at the fire-scarred effigies of the old knights.

Almost all old churches in Britain, certainly those built before about AD 1500, are secret repositories of pagan symbolism and ancient power. Because some New Pagans reject the Christian faith they also throw out the heritage, preserved in stone in many a village church, because of its new religious context. They should be willing to open their eyes and see with the simplicity of their country-dwelling forebears the hidden messages revealed by carvings and decorated windows, adorning the interior heights and the exterior pinnacles of old chapels in the green countryside.

Most older churches are aligned with the altar in the East, the first point blessed in both pagan and Christian ceremonies. In fact, the altar end of many old churches points at the place of sunrise on the day of the saint to whom the edifice is consecrated. Many early saints were, in fact, Celtic guardian spirits, or pagan gods and goddesses thinly disguised. A little research into the ancestry of the saint to whom your nearest old church is dedicated might provide some fascinating revelation! The North door was nearly always blocked up, and in some cases was known as the 'Devil's Door', mainly, I suppose, because a chill North wind blowing through it would benefit neither priest nor congregation. But to the pagan the North was a sacred direction and it is here, often on the outside of the church, that many pagan carvings or symbols will be seen to this day. These range from the heads of cats, deer or bears to the vast array of Green Men, foliate heads or zodiacal symbols.

On the towers or spires, well out of the way of the common view, there are the faces of gargoyles, known delightfully in Somerset as 'Hunky-punks', again often basically animals or small demons, tongue-pokers or hybrid man-creatures, sometimes with exaggerated sexual parts. The famous 'Sheelah-na-gigs' turn up too, from time to time, showing the Goddess in her birth-giving or wildly erotic aspect. The name, from Irish Gaelic, has never been fully understood, but the name of the British goddess Sul or Sulis, worshipped at Bath,

the Roman 'Aquae Sulis', also means 'eye' or 'opening' and
may well arise from the same concept. At Bath, the only hot
spring in Britain gushes forth, red-stained in the sacred
enclosure, and is visited by millions of unknowing pilgrims at
the very ancient Goddess Shrine every year. It was known for
its oracle and healing power long before the Romans came and
set up their huge temple there, with its official haruspex, the
State diviner.

Around the country, and all over Europe, you will find traces
of the Old Gods wherever you look. Perhaps the most common,
occurring not only in many village churches and city cathedrals
but on ordinary Victorian houses and as a public house name or
sign, is the Green Man. This is the witches' God, he who is the
Lord of Growing Things, known in folklore as Jack-in-the-
Green, Robin Goodfellow and even Robin Hood. His face is
partly made up of leaves, fruit, grapes or trails of foliage
issuing, like the words he has never spoken, from his mouth, or
entwined in his hair and beard. He is the Son of Pan, that
Greek God of all wild things, and has the same pointed ears,
older visage and smiling expression.

Not only is he found all over minor buildings but there are
many town halls, university buildings and theatres where his
laughing face may be seen, peering from its leafy surrounds.
Many of these carvings were quite recent for this particular
image seems to have somehow appealed to the Victorians. Of
course, they often decorated their municipal edifices with
classical figures, goddesses and gods associated with art, music,
law or commerce. Why this pagan face appears so frequently in
that elite company is not clear, yet on elegant public buildings
in many a city centre, moulded in plaster, carved in stone,
shaped in brick or tile, the Green Man is to be found
throughout the land. The power of the wild aspect of Nature, so
often absent from inner cities and great housing estates seems to
have caused his older presence to be felt, and inspired masons,
architects and builders to include him among their thronging
buildings.

Do really look at the long rows of terraced houses, and see if
over the doors or at the tops of the windows or incorporated as
decorative details on the faces of houses you can find this
smiling old God of Nature. As well as his head there are often
goddesses with crescent moons in their hair, or regal Mother
Natures smiling down on passers by. Also the decoration on

either side of the windows often shows some of the sacred birds, beasts or flowers long associated with pagan themes. I have never found Christian traces used in similar ways, or decking out so many houses in the vast estates which sprang up to accommodate the workers in the early part of the nineteenth century. You will often find really beautiful brick or tile mouldings of apples and pomegranates, both sacred to the Goddess in the Greek and Celtic traditions, roses, lilies, sunflowers and laurel, whose leaves were chewed to inspire the ancient oracles. The birds depicted in low relief often represent ravens or wrens, skylarks or herons, all, in their own way, sacred to the Old Gods.

The Green Man, as well as being quite a common pub name, is a character who turns up in many of the surviving country or seasonal customs. For example, in Abbots Bromley in Staffordshire, a group of green-clad dancers perform an extremely old dance early in September each year. Most of the dancers carry sets of reindeer antlers, long extinct in that part of the country, some of which have been carbon-dated to around AD 1000. This does not guarantee that the dance has an unbroken tradition going back a thousand or more years, but it seems very likely. In earlier times the area was a forest and so deer hunting with bows and arrows, which forms a part of the modern dance, was a natural activity thereabouts. Also, like many similar dances in other places, the symbolic killing of an animal or 'hobby horse' usually depicts the overcoming of the darkness of winter, or harm to garnered crops, rather than some sort of animal sacrifice.

In other places the Green Man is part of the retinue of the May Queen, nearly always a young girl, dressed in the White Goddess's colour, decked with flowers and ribbons, who is accompanied by Robin Hood or the Forest King. Sometimes the Green Man is made up as a giant, covered with a framework of wire or branches interwoven with early leaves or flowers. Sometimes he walks through the village or rides around the boundaries, marking out an ancient territory. In South Queensferry on the Firth of Forth the Burryman comes forth, completely covered with the clinging green burrs of the burdock plant, and slowly parades about with two flower-topped wands in his outstretched hands, looking very like the far greater Green Man carved into the chalk hillside at Wilmington in Sussex. In many other annual, local processions there are

green-clad fellows, always linked with a pagan past, when the
carrying of green branches or flower garlands was the best way
in which the country folk could celebrate the turning cycle of the
agricultural year.

The Romans accused the Druids, those mysterious Celtic
priests, of burning people in wicker baskets, as many people
will have seen in the film *The Wicker Man*, but in reality it
wouldn't have worked. It is far more likely that the Druids did
indeed make wicker or woven figures covered with leaves or
flowers, which were cast onto a fire or into the sea, or left to
decay in a sacred grove, as an offering to the powers of the
Elements. Today we still have the variety of corn dollies or kern
kings, woven from the last sheaf of wheat, oats or barley, and
bound with blood-red ribbons, signifying the life force still
contained therein. In different places there are special patterns,
depicting a traditional concept of the Corn Spirit. These are
found in Britain, all over Europe, in India, Greece and South
America.

It really is worth going to see any traditional customs which
may be celebrated in your area or where you spend your
holiday, for the wild pagan spirit has survived in a surprising
number of places, and is demonstrating its power of life
overcoming death in an enormous variety of different regional
forms. There are plenty of books on calendar customs and folk
festivals; many will be in the library. Whether just the local
Morris side, dancing their weather magic with hankies or their
male fertility magic with sticks, or the ritual dances with long or
rapper swords, they are the latest inheritors of a long-surviving
tradition of white-clad dancers celebrating in the open air.
Their bells ward off harm, their bright ribbons and flowers ask
blessings of the Old Ones, their white clothes are worn in
honour of the White Goddess, Maiden of Spring, fruitful Earth
Mother in the long summer days. Even their name, Morris,
may be derived from that other sacred Mother, Mary, and they
are Mary's Men! Women are taking up some of these dances,
but their own dances were different, performed in family
groups, with spindles, winnowing sieves or domestic brooms
rather than sticks, and they danced in honour of the Moon
Goddess. These dances could be recalled, by far memory or
remembering past lives.

Many dances today begin outside, or occasionally inside,
some of the ancient churches. This may seem strange, but often

those were the old pagan sacred sites, and at least a small
church is better than a large supermarket on such holy ground.
You will know the antiquity and sacredness of such places by
the circular churchyard wall, for example, or the aged yew tree,
which has little connection with bow-making or any other
mundane purpose. Yews were sacred to the Dark Goddess, the
Taker to Rest, and they may well have been there long before
the church was built. If you find an old church with a great
yew, look also for the remains of standing stones built into the
walls, or in the surrounding enclosure. Look too, perhaps with
binoculars, at the faces carved on the North wall, or the tower
or spire. Walk slowly round, feeling the energies, the power
lines unaltered by the newer edifice. Examine the porch, any
faces over the door, the angular masons' marks cut into the
stone, often including the magical five-pointed star or
pentagram, so popular with modern witches who may well not
appreciate its ancient significance.

Venture inside, with a quiet prayer to all Holy Mothers and
all sacrificed God-Sons, and look for the symbols of power. The
roof bosses, acting like wheel hubs in the roof beams, are often
carved or painted wood or stone, and these are the most
common places for pagan or other symbols to be seen. Many
have dragons, mazes, the heads of wild animals and magical
flowers. You will find goddesses smiling down at you, or Green
Men with their foliate faces, leafy beards, fruiting hair. You
may find goats, unicorns, mermaids, especially as carvings on
pew ends of seaside village churches, or as misericords, hidden
under upturned seats in the vast and lofty cathedrals, those
ancient centres of power. Remember, most of the masons,
carvers and builders were members of secret brotherhoods, just
as much a Craft Guild as were the witches. Each in their own
way found methods to preserve their holy symbols, their own
mythology, their own animals and trees of power.

Not only did the Church unknowingly preserve the faces of
the Old Gods in their roofs and towers, but they also kept the
ancient pre-Christian festivals. One of the early Church Fathers
insisted that new churches were built in places where the people
were accustomed to go to worship on their older feasts, which is
why small lonely chapels exist on many an uninhabited hilltop,
or in remote valleys. Many of these high churches are dedicated
to St Michael who took on many of the aspects of the earlier Sun
God. Michaelmas is around the Autumnal Equinox when day

and night are equal, and Michael is a saint who interacts with
the power of darkness, seen in the newer faith as the Devil. St
Michael, unlike St George who is another solar-type saint, does
not slay his adversary but overcomes him. Thus the Light-
bringer, Lucifer, is balanced with the Lord of Fire, St Michael.
In the spring this pattern is reversed.

Keeping holy the ancient high places, using their magical or
healing springs (a frequent feature of old chapels is a water well
of some sort) in the new religion, celebrating harvests, wakes,
gatherings and partings in the traditionally sacred places, has
allowed us, two or four or ten thousand years later, to be
reminded of those things which were blessed or magical. Take
off the blinkers which prevent you considering any part of the
newer faiths, and underneath their dark surface you will see the
green fire of Mother Nature's own religion, its sacred centres,
its holy days, preserved and shining. The Goddess never dies;
she cannot die for she is the Bringer of Life, just as the God is
the Bringer of Light.

Exercises

You will need to spend at least fifteen to twenty minutes every
day you can in some sort of meditation practice. You can do it
whilst walking, or doing mundane tasks, waiting for transport
or commuting, as well as at deliberately set aside moments at
the start or end of your day. Choose aspects of the gods, folk or
hero tales, symbols or even the odd bits of information all your
research will dredge up as themes. Write down whatever you
discover, for your researches may prove very valuable.

During the sixth moon you will need to look for survivals all
round you, many, indeed, almost under your nose. Put aside
any misconceptions and go and explore a local old church or
historical monument. Try to see it as it was when first built, and
think about the folk who worked at it.

Try to find out what the oldest local construction is, and if
archaeologists have ever dug in your area. Reports of ancient
findings will be in the reference library. Search the nearest
museum for old artefacts or traditional happenings, perhaps
now no more. What pagan traces can you find there?

Make a Green Man mask, using leaves on a thin card base –
if it happens to be winter, make the leaves from green card, or

paint them on. See if you can discover anything about the
'Mask Prayer' said by some pagans as they changed into their
magical personality. Try to write such an invocation, asking for
help to become your magical self.

Who was the goddess most closely associated with the Green
Man? Make a mask or garland to represent her magical powers.

Do they have a maypole in your area, and do the local
schoolchildren elect a May Queen or King? Is there a turf maze
or a hedge labyrinth? Using an equal-armed cross with a dot at
each quarter, draw a unicursal maze. You can make these big
enough to walk round, marking the walls with string or lawn
mowings!

Find out how to make corn dollies – handicrafts shops sell kits
or books of instructions. These can also be made of lavender
stalks, and varieties of rushes, which can be woven to make St
Bridget's Cross.

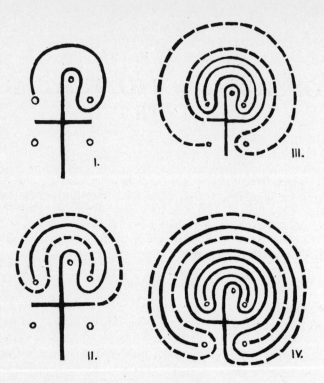

Try tying a knot in a narrow strip of paper and carefully flattening the resulting knot, until it is an even shape. Why is this a Witch's Secret? What use can you make of such a pattern?

Here are some more books to sample or collect:

Ralph Whitlock, *In Search of Lost Gods* (Phaidon Press)
Brian Branston, *The Lost Gods of England* (Thames and Hudson)
Janet and Colin Bord, *Mysterious Britain* (Garnstone Press)
Diana Carey and Judy Large, *Festivals, Family and Food* (Hawthorn Press)
Marian Green, *The Elements of Natural Magic* (Element Books)
Paul Devereux, *Places of Power* (Blandford Press)

7.
CONSIDERING THE HEALING ARTS

The practice of conventional medicine was found to be more conveniently managed if the body was treated as a collection of parts rather than as an indivisible whole. Alternative medicine is now the guardian of an approach to health that claims that no part of the body can be made better unless the underlying cause is also discovered and treated . . .

John Lloyd Fraser: *The Medicine Men*

Before you begin with any sort of healing methods, even if you intend only to experiment upon yourself, you should consider very thoroughly the whole ethical situation, and realise that the knowledge of healing carries with it a very heavy responsibility. It might seem to be an excellent and commendable application of magical knowledge, in that you can offer healing arts to everyone around you, but consider.

In the ebb and flow of ordinary life people are being taught lessons, given training and hidden guidance as to how best to carry on their lives. Illness, as a subject of debate in psychological circles, is now being seen in a new light. It is sometimes considered as a 'teaching condition' rather than purely a discomfort or disruption to everyday life. A whole new aspect of health and disease is being looked at in that illnesses only strike us if we let them. This might seem a curious statement; after all, no one really wants to be ill, do they? Look at it from a different angle. Being ill will permit you to take time off from a boring or perhaps stressful lifestyle; it will permit you to seek sympathy, help or comfort from those around you who perhaps take your activities for granted. Illness offers an opportunity to rest, to lie in bed longer than normal, to sleep, to be pampered, to eat chosen dishes rather than what the rest of the household prefers.

On a grander scale, it is considered by some psychologists that illness is a way of rebalancing our karmic debts. If we have harmed others in previous lives, the hurt they suffered comes to us as the pain of an illness or the disability of disease, rather than as direct action from them in their current life. If we have been tyrants or torturers, cruel slavedrivers or even brutal to animals, perhaps this is how we are taught valuable lessons. I don't accept that all illnesses are brought upon us by our wishing or permitting them to attack us, but certainly in some instances, when all things are fully considered, there is a factor of rebalancing karma to be considered. After all, the viruses and bacteria of most diseases are in the air around us every day. The stresses or chemical cocktails which may trigger changes in our bodies leading to cancers or arthritis will touch us as well as our neighbours who actually become ill with such disorders.

Do give these concepts a good deal of thought before you start trying any arts of healing. Think too about anything which you have suffered from in the last few years. When did it start? Was anything going on in your life which might have made you more vulnerable then? Have any of your family been ill because of their attitude to you, or your treatment of them?

Healing can take many forms, from a complete and speedy recovery from whatever ill the patient is suffering from, to an ongoing condition for which there can be no physical recovery, yet spiritual insight and a vast improvement in the quality of life may ensue. Some diseases or accidents can increase the sufferer's perception about the value of a normal life, a greater understanding of handicap or disability, and so a far greater sympathy with others disabled in a similar way. Sometimes it is just a deeper understanding of the concept of 'health' or 'healing' and an expanded awareness of how multifaceted this idea may be. Every such experience will have all sorts of effects on the sufferer, and such matters must be taken into account by those who might come to offer healing or advice.

The important aspect of any form of health counselling or healing arts is that of treating the whole person, not just the painful area or symptoms. The holistic view underpins many of the alternative therapies which have become popular and more readily available in the last few years. These include homoeopathy, spiritual healing, aromatherapy, reflexology, herbalism and naturopathic medicine. Acupuncture and its associated forms of shiatsu, Touch for Health and even massage all treat the entire individual. Many of these healing arts, inherited from Far Eastern sources, acknowledge that everyone has a basic life force called *ch'i* which contains two components, Yin and Yang, positive and negative, male and female. Illness, pain or discomfort may be caused by a disruption of this essential flow of *ch'i*, or life energy. Sometimes there is too little Yin and too much Yang, or vice versa, or perhaps the courses through which this energy flows, called meridians in English, are blocked or expanded. It is by applying very fine needles or pressure to certain points along these meridians that the energy is allowed to resume its balanced flow, healing not only the immediate pain or disease, but the whole patient, body and soul.

From another angle, recent research is showing us new things about the sensitivity of the human organism. Tests are indicating that people can actually detect invisible energies like radioactivity and ultrasound, and changes in the Earth's magnetic field. These unexpected results have been found by scientists examining the positions of ancient stone circles as part of the Dragon Project. It is becoming clearer that the sorts of stones used in these monuments, their positions and the places in which they have been erected are all important, and show uncommon variations in natural levels of background radiation, for example, or strange pulses of ultrasound or magnetic anomalies. The researchers are convinced that the ancient people who set up the alignments were in some way aware of these variations, and used them to position or select the sites and materials used in them.

Just as people were sensitive to such unconsciously detected forces in the ancient world, they would certainly be sensitive to the increased doses put out by the activities of civilisation. This may be the underlying cause of many recurrent illnesses, or mental or physical conditions which appear to defy the healing powers of modern medicine. The constant exposure to unnatural forces, low dose radiation both natural and caused by the nuclear industry, the chemical cocktails we consume along with our food and drink, the pollution in the very air we breathe, all are going to do us no good, and many may do actual harm, possibly resulting in cancers, bone and blood conditions which are very difficult to treat. Again, recent studies have shown that some forms of radiation can affect the children of fathers working in hazardous places, leading, perhaps, to an increased

risk of leukaemia, or other serious conditions. The greatest
problem is that we simply do not know what we may be exposed
to throughout our lives!

Although the kind of medicine and healing practised by the
old village witches probably did not cover the problems of
today's world, nearly all the known treatments were holistic.
Herbal medicine works on the entire person, not just the
immediate area to which it is applied. Some forms of treatment
act not only on the physical body but on the more subtle etheric
level. (The etheric field around people is visible to most trained
witches who look, in low light, at bare flesh against a dark
background. A narrow band of energy can be clearly seen. You
can experiment by looking at your reflection in a mirror,
concentrating around the edges of your skin against a lighter, or
perhaps darker, plain background.) Beyond the narrow etheric,
some people can train themselves to see the wide-spreading,
rainbow-coloured filaments of the aura proper. This too can be
an excellent indication of health and energy levels, being both
brighter and larger in a well and balanced person than in a
weary or sick one. If you start to see auras clearly, when in a
relaxed and meditative state, do remember that you are also
looking through your own aura, and the colour you may see
around someone else will be a combination of your colours and
theirs. Look at the shape of the aura (which can be detected by
dowsing even by those who cannot see it), how far it reaches
upwards, how stripy or blotched with darker patches or specific
colours, or spirals of lightness. Some books try to attribute
particular meanings to each of these features, but most people
have very individual patterns and colours, so hard and fast rules
should not necessarily be applied. Once you learn to detect this
energy field around living people, animals, trees or even special
stones, you will intuitively be guided to understand the
significance of what you can see or sense.

You should try to learn control of your psychic senses at the
same time as you are experimenting with seeing auras or
sensing power about sacred sites, for it is possible to be too
sensitive. If you are not able to 'deliberately switch off' your
sensitivity you may begin to find that your nerves become
jangled and you start to feel oppressed in the presence of
strangers. This is just a matter of asking that your inner senses
be under your own control. Traditionally, witches and
magicians use a simple ritual, which is nearly always of a

mental nature, to surround themselves with a fragile shell of temporary protection. In some older books novices are instructed to perform heavy banishing rituals about themselves, but these wipe away all human contacts and, rather than making the individual feel safer, make him feel extremely sensitive and vulnerable. You only need to ask the Protective Goddess or the Guardian God to watch over you, or awaken your Higher Self to prevent your newly expanded senses from being overwhelmed, whilst gradually allowing you to adjust to greater skills and feelings as you become more experienced.

In the old days the villagers relied completely on the skills of the Wise Woman or Cunning Man to see them into the world, to help with illness or accidents, to heal their cattle or sheep, to improve the fertility of their land, to mend broken hearts, wreak revenge on enemies, to see into the future, and finally to see that their dead were decently laid out for burial. Many of these aspects of the traditional crafts are now dealt with by a variety of trained people, but certainly helping with minor complaints, sorting out affairs of the heart, looking into the future or the past to help enquirers learn from their experiences, still fall well within the competence of many modern witches and magicians. Also, if you are willing and able to undergo proper training in herbalism, reflexology, hypnotherapy, aromatherapy, massage or homoeopathy, you will be using more recent methods, yet still treading in the healing footsteps of your forebears.

Do be discreet about your knowledge of healing, or of divination come to that, for it is very easy for fools to rush in where angels might fear to tread. If you let on at work that you know something about healing you may well be inundated with requests which could be beyond your competence, if you are still learning the arts. Some people might expect miraculous effects, or prefer to take an amateur's advice or treatment, rather than seeking orthodox diagnosis or treatment. It is always best, except in very minor ills like colds or influenza, bruises and tiredness, to suggest that the sufferer gets expert advice before being exposed to whichever alternative therapy you happen to be learning. Certainly you can experiment on yourself but as you get your life under control, begin to gain insights and inspiration as to your path in life and access to those inner powers, you will probably improve your health, if it needed improvement, as you go.

The more magical forms of healing used by the Old Wise Ones include what might be called spiritual healing, the laying on of hands, distant healing and pure esoteric healing, possibly using a magical talisman or verbal spell. In every case you must follow some basic rules. First you *must* be asked to help by the patient or someone responsible for them if it is a child, for example. Secondly, try to find out exactly what is wrong with them, and if they haven't seen a doctor yet feel some sort of external healing agency needs to be applied, do encourage them to get at least a professional diagnosis. That could save their lives, if they are seriously ill! Thirdly, tell them that you can only *help* them to get better – you are not the Creative Force, and they must work towards their own recovery, not simply rely on you, or a doctor, to cure them. Fourthly, go into the circumstances of their illness with them, seeing if there is an external reason for their condition, like their lifestyle, bad habits, stress from a job or family situation, or simply that they really need rest or a change of circumstances and being 'ill' is as good an excuse for having a few days off work as anything.

Try to get their cooperation in whatever you intend to do for them, obviously after you have received some training in the method. If you intend to use magic, spells or a talisman, do explain to them, as some people can be very shocked at the idea of 'witchcraft', often still seen as a series of evil arts, being applied to their health. You can make things worse if a patient is led into an incense-filled room, where strange words are chanted over him and mystical symbols marked on his sore stomach with holy oil. You can scare people by being too physical as well; someone unused to being touched by other people, could find the experience of having his feet massaged, as in reflexology, a bit too weird! After all, you do want to help those who request healing, not scare the wits out of them.

If the sick person is there in person, you may be able to burn gold candles to request that the healing power of the sun may shine upon him, but actual sunshine will be just as effective. You may be able to massage away pain, or lay your hands upon him and ask that the restorative power of the Goddess or the God be felt through your touch, or you may simply counsel him on a more healthy lifestyle, while silently asking that healing flow into him. If your partner cannot be there in person, you might act on a photograph or that earlier version, a wax image, which was far more often used for healing than harming, but you must still be specifically asked for help. Use your increased power of imagination, by seeing him well and happy. Make a talisman on a gold circle, calling on the health-giving power of the sun to lighten his burden, and bring him increased energy.

You can use the power of the waxing moon to aid a person's strength and resistance to disease, and the waning power to wipe away the pain, distress or complications, so that at any time you may begin your treatment. Always use your own psychic powers to discover where the real seat of any illness lies, rather than just treating symptoms, and ask that they understand the meaning of their illness. Because the moon rules our mental state, and almost all diseases have a mental component, in that a sufferer may simply be frightened at being ill, or he may be sick because he is so stressed or anxious that he catches something nasty, using her changing light in the healing will add an extra benefit.

Learn to be able to take your own pulse in your wrist or neck, gently, so that you can detect how much more or less relaxed you are after a meditation or ritual celebration. Teach yourself the simple art of brewing herb teas for calmness or energy. Study the uses of aromatic oils, incenses (which have always been an important aspect of the use of herbs), gums and resins. Find a supplier who will sell pure incense gums so that you can try each in turn, to see if you like the smell when you burn it on the special charcoal blocks. Make sure you don't use too much, about half a teaspoon is plenty to try, on half a charcoal block. Some incenses give off thick smoke and can make you cough, others may make your eyes run.

Some illnesses have a very great psychological effect, and it was to combat this that Dr Edward Bach, working in the 1940s, developed his collection of potent flower remedies. Today, there are 38 used in Britain, but the USA and other places have developed expanded lists, using local herbs, trees and plants. These gentle remedies work by using what medieval herbalists called the 'virtue' of certain trees, flowers, shrubs or herbs. Various parts of the plants are immersed in spring water, in sunlight, and preserved usually by the addition of a little brandy. They do not work directly on physical illnesses, but on the mental conditions which may underlie the problem. For example, if a child is frightened of failing an exam he may complain of a tummy ache or feeling sick. The flower remedy would work on the underlying fear rather than the expressed symptoms. Similarly, many adults suffer mental states, mild or severe, that can manifest as bodily illness. In each case there is a specific plant which will quite slowly and gently alleviate the condition, allowing the strength of that person's character to overcome the actual disease or distress. These remedies are now widely available from good chemists, or health food shops or homoeopathic pharmacies. Some New Age centres also have specialists in the use of these Bach Remedies who can be consulted, or even run short courses about their effects and uses.

Do be aware, though, that many apparently simple forms of medicine or therapy can be very powerful even in the hands of the inexperienced. In aromatherapy, the essential oils which are vaporised, used in massage oil or applied to certain places on the body can be too strong, and some cause reactions in certain people. Do seek out some sort of training, and be willing to stick to one or two systems until you are really competent. Learn about your own health, looking at every accident or serious illness you have suffered. Think back to the circumstances, the mental and spiritual as well as the physical situation that existed at the time.

Be willing to spend some time in meditation upon the triple concept of mind and body and spirit, for illness, both in yourself and others, may begin in any one of these areas. Today, we have lost our contact with the spiritual aspects of our lives, a loss that is not usually clearly felt, except perhaps by those who are seeking some sort of fundamental religious experience, often itself a clear sign of *dis-ease* within them. Many people have come to see that material comfort, even wealth, does not totally fulfil them, and that there is sometimes a deep longing for something which cannot be defined, so is all the harder to seek out. Carl Jung recognised the power of this inner yearning, making the religious impulse as important as the sexual as one of the underlying drives which direct our actions. We all need goals to strive towards, and those who have become satisfied with a kindly partner, a good and rewarding job, a comfortable home still reach out for something else. Often these people are the ones who fall prey to the unscrupulous, selling some 'philosophy' or 'cult' to the unwary for a fat sum of money. What you should discover for yourself is that spiritual riches can only be gained by personal effort and the sweat of your own brow.

Most of the old-fashioned virtues are gifts of the spirit, like sympathy, patience, the ability to listen and comfort, becoming inwardly still and hearing the voice of the God/Goddess within for guidance or help. It only requires that you become a seeker after good, in whatever way you may define that concept. Reach out towards the best within your heart, the strengths that you do not yet recognise, the inner peace and tranquility which, once you have realised it for yourself, can easily and freely be passed on to others around you. Learn to know that all round you, invisibly, there are 'angels' or powers who will listen, hear your requests and offer assistance, if you give them credence. This communication is vital if you are setting out to offer healing to others for it will advise when you can help, and warn when you would be wiser to hold back. It requires that you learn trust, both of your own growing abilities and of that silent voice inside your head which will gladly instruct and guide, if you are perplexed.

Relaxation is by far the most healing art you can learn, or share with others. It is an essential part of all magical work, for power can only be handled safely by one who is at peace and still within themselves because it will push against any resistance and cause discomfort. If you can train yourself to relax every muscle, starting from your feet, you will gain a valuable skill.

Sit in a comfortable but supportive chair, with your back straight and your head upright. Clench your toes for a pulse beat of three, then relax them, then the muscles under your foot; your ankles; your calves; knees and thighs; and all those great muscles in your stomach and bottom. Pull them in tightly for a count of three, and then let them relax totally so that you can feel no tension anywhere. Continue with the muscles between your ribs, taking a deep breath and counting three and releasing it. Work thoroughly through all the tensions in your shoulders, neck, along your arms, your wrists and fingers, letting these take up a relaxed, slightly curled position on your knees or the arms of the chair. Pause and sense through every part of your body, again tensing and loosening anywhere where you detect stress. Finally, consider your face and the muscles behind your ears and in your scalp. Make faces, stretch open your eyes and mouth, wiggle your jaw, flex your neck, frown and wrinkle up your lips, then let the whole lot relax totally, gently closing your eyes.

The next part of this healing exercise is to ensure that your

head feels balanced on your neck. You can train yourself to
meditate or enter any of the magical states of mind with your
head held upright. Tell it to stay put so that it doesn't impede
your breathing, or roll to one side and disturb your mood. If
you are meditating, your head will stay put; if you are
slumbering, dozing or cheating, it will probably slump!

Next dedicate a few moments to your breathing. In most
magical states this tends to slow down, so you can help the
relaxation along by deliberately taking slow, deep breaths. If
you can feel your own pulse in your wrist use that as an aid to
this exercise, breathing in as you count ten beats, holding for
six, breathing out for ten, holding out for six. This sort of thing
is much harder to do than to read about, for it takes that other
vital magical skill, concentration. Try it!

You need to be able to take at least ten long, slow breaths,
using the 10:6:10:6 counts without strain (you might find you
need to count more than ten, or perhaps less if you are not very
well) as this will also help you relax. On its own this slow deep
breathing can be very calming, and if you are under stress at
work, or have to attend an interview, or go to the dentist, this
simple relaxing procedure can save a lot of pain and distress. As
you breathe out imagine a tide of pain, trouble or 'darkness',
which represents anything you wish to get rid of, being
breathed out like chimney smoke, to be dissipated into a clear
sky, and a fresh cool draught of sunlight being breathed in,
entering every part of you, to refresh and strengthen your inner
self.

The third part of this valuable exercise is the mental aspect.
Here you should focus your inner sight on a pleasing,
unstructured scene. A garden of bright flowers, the sea washing
onto a smooth, sandy beach, the wind in the grass or soft clouds
drifting across a summer sky; any of these or something which
is comforting and gentle should occupy your mind's eye.
Again, be relaxed and if only colours or vague shapes will come,
accept that. You are trying to be at rest not creating difficult
images to play with. Gradually you will notice, as the various
stages of this useful experiment unfold, that your mind is feeling
peaceful and dreamy, time has ceased and you are comfortable
and warm. Begin to drift, simply watching not merely the
pictures in your mind, but how you feel, how ideas are flowing
past your point of awareness, or even that there is a delightful
blankness and sensation of detachment. You have total control

over this state and so long as you are content it will, with a fair bit of practice, remain around you. Now is the time to begin to look at any health problems you have, seeking not the symptom but the root cause. You may sense the position of an old injury, or recall an event which led to some buried bad feelings which have caused you to have a 'pain in the neck'. You may realise that something you do to other people, seen as a vague colour or shape, is making you unwell. Again, try it and see what you can discover.

It is also a valuable exercise to lead a friend through this same technique, watching how they take up a relaxed (or even still tensed) position, seeing how their face relaxes and they sink into the warmth of calmness. You may see their eyeballs moving under their closed lids as they scan the peaceful scene you describe. Notice how their breathing changes, slows and may seem very shallow, because similar things should be happening to you, but your awareness of them will not be very clear. Repeat any parts of the muscle relaxation sequence if you can see tension anywhere, and if they find this whole process very strange, stop at the point where they have got their faces relaxed, gently telling them to open their eyes and see how much better they feel. This alone can cure tension headaches, stiff necks and tired shoulders. It is good for weary eyes worn out by staring at VDUs all day, too, or too much TV!

If you have tried with a healthy friend a few times, you can feel confident if you are trying to help someone who is actually ill. You lead them to the very relaxed and detached state and then very carefully ask them about their illness. When it began, if they caught it from someone else, if they have had it before and, if so, how long it took to go away. Always keep the questions slow, gentle and lighthearted. It is not a time for heavy amateur psychoanalysis, but a careful encouragement of the individual's relaxed frame of mind which might be able to divulge the real reason for their current state of discomfort. Even if you aren't getting results that way, you can suggest that they use their own healing powers, that they will discover what makes them feel better, what helps and what hinders. Allow this thought to sink in thoroughly, then gently lead them back to full awareness, still, hopefully, feeling a bit more relaxed and calm.

When you have mastered the more advanced skills of magical working you can, with a suitable patient, carry out this relaxation technique within your magical circle, invoking the healing power of the Sun God, or the Goddess of Healing to assist them. You can prepare a talisman using the information which they have given you about the roots of their illness, warding off stress, accidents or bacteria, applying your knowledge of the powers, colours, numbers and other symbolism of the planets.

If you are willing to use healing techniques upon yourself you will quickly be able to help others from your own experience. By gaining knowledge and experience first, and also opening up through methods like relaxation, you will add further dimensions to book learning or practical instruction. All your healing and magical knowledge should go hand in hand. You will realise that as you learn more about Nature, she will teach you how all sorts of ordinary things can be added to your therapeutic repertoire. You will learn which things work best for the body, which for the mind and, most important in this hectic day and age, which assist with the spiritual discomforts many of us suffer from. The underlying problems will always be causes rather than symptoms. If a limb is broken then splinting it carefully will go a long way to alleviate the pain; if someone is unhappy and that is giving them stomach trouble or heart ache, you are dealing with a different dimension of disturbance, which, as in the old days, the village witch is capable of coping with.

Each day, seek a time of quiet, walking or sitting or resting, when you can talk to the Goddess, who certainly will be with you in your everyday round of work and relaxation. Now you can ask for healing, or if you are concerned about someone else, guidance as to what best to do for them. You may be inspired to make them a posy of flowers, write a poem, or a song. You might know that it is time for them to learn unaided some lesson about their lifestyle or past follies. You might even realise that no matter what you wish to happen, it is time for them, young or old, to pass on to a new life.

Allowing those who had completed their life span to pass on was also traditionally a matter for the wise woman or man; it is far more healthy to accept that a life is due to end and that peace and understanding should fall upon the person. If you accept, as many pagans do, that we all live many lives, it is really no worse than changing schools or moving house. Those who are not comforted by such a concept will find death more difficult to deal with, for they will feel pain, grief, and loss, just as you will, but knowing the essential spirit of a loved one will return after a due rest is a very beneficial point of view. Many people, losing a close friend or relative, feel anger and a sense of outrage that their loved one has died and not them, but the Lords of Karma are not cruel. No one is taken out of life if they have things to do which will not wait. There is a logic, beyond human ken perhaps, but whatever happens, the Goddess, Giver of Life and of Rest, is leading that soul further on its journey towards the Light. Be strong and calm yourself, if you are able to be with the dying person, and tell them about the great adventure they may soon set out upon. Give them mental comfort, and pray that they have a gentle passing, in sleep.

If someone is dying and you are not there, light a new white candle and ask the Goddess to gently take them into her arms and bring them to the Garden of the Soul, where friends and loved ones will meet again. As the candle burns down, often the soul departs with a smile on their face, as if they can see the Light and those they love waiting.

Exercises

How much you need to study will depend on your own ordinary state of health. If you are always well, then your healing studies may need to be applied to others. If you suffer frequent colds, allergies, headaches, back pain or general ill health, you will need to begin your practical work by considering what makes you unwell and what remedies or forms of alternative therapy you are willing to try. In your Book of Illumination list all the occasions in the last year when you were ill and, if you can recall, what was going on in your life which might have contributed to the situation. If you have been generally healthy, decide why.

List a number of forms of therapy and what they consist of, trying to find holistic methods. Consider if you would like to learn one, and if so discover the training body which teaches it or, if it is a subject you can master alone, a book that will help you.

Learn to take your own pulse, in your wrist or throat, so that you can use this for 'biofeedback', taking your pulse rate before and after meditation or concentration exercises, or even after rituals or divination sessions. Count your breaths, and learn to concentrate on breathing slowly in and out whilst counting sets of pulse beats, so that you are unaware of anything else. Teach yourself to do this for two minutes and practise until you can concentrate for five minutes.

Start growing or collecting herbs, both for cooking (even if you happen to be someone who doesn't cook for yourself) and for healing and incense, dream improvement or relaxation. Try at least four different herb teas to see what they do for you.

Experiment with different forms of relaxation for meditation, for example sitting still, walking, lying on your back or side, slumped in an easy chair or whilst doing boring tasks, when your mind can free-wheel around a topic. See which produces the most useful results.

Make a talisman for healing some aspect of the Earth as a whole, or that wisdom in the use of natural resources will dawn on those in power. Try to make it out of biodegradable materials, and bury it in a sacred place.

Discuss ill health with friends or the family. Get their views on the psychology of illness and wellbeing.

Start studying with a school or training scheme, even evening classes if you can, so that you have some serious instruction about a healing method. Keep quiet about your budding skills, or you may get more patients than you can handle!

There are many hundreds of excellent instructional and explanatory books on dozens of different alternative therapies or holistic healing methods so do check the library catalogue. After all, the old village witches were famed for their healing skills, using primitive methods.

Murry Hope, *The Psychology of Healing* (Element Books)
Michael Howard, *Traditional Folk Remedies* (Century)
Alice A Bailey, *Esoteric Healing* (Lucis Press)
Carl and Stephanie Simonton, *Getting Well Again* (Tarcher)
Larry Dossey, *Space, Time and Medicine* (Shambhala)
Fritjof Capra, *The Turning Point* (Wildwood House)

8.

THE OLD CRAFTS OF
DIVINATION AND DOWSING

You could use a picture or a pattern as an analogy to represent
something. In this sense there is a lot of similarity between using a
pendulum and using one of the classic divinatory tools such as the
Tarot or the I Ching. The main difference is that with the
pendulum we're specifically asking a single question and aiming
for a single answer, whereas with the Tarot we're using the rich
symbolism of the card designs, developed over centuries, as
allegories rather than analogies, to look at a general background in
an overall way. Again, it's like the pendulum, 'entirely
coincidence and mostly imaginary' . . . to be used rather than
worried about.

Tom Graves: *The Elements of Pendulum Dowsing*

Among the many skills the old village witches had was that of
divination in its many forms. Technically, divination is a
method of receiving information directly from the divinity,
which in both ancient and modern practice takes many forms.
The older folk forms for telling people's fortunes include
palmistry, when the lines and shapes of the hands are
considered; reading the messages of cards, particularly the
magical images imparted by the Tarot cards, whose history
may well be extremely old although the decks we are familiar
with today only came into use from about AD 1500. The old
wise women and men could read omens, a much ignored
system about which I will explain later, for this is a very simple
method relying entirely on unstructured intuition.

It is likely that the Old Wise Ones had a basic knowledge of
astrology, not the intellectual, ephemeris-based system used
by most modern astrologers, but a reaction to the actual
positions of the planets and signs as they appeared in the night
sky. Oracle stones, marked on one side with traditional, planet-

based symbols, were tossed out onto the floor, and their message read from the position and relationship of each visible pattern by those wise in this matter. More complex versions of this old method are beginning to appear commercially, using the Scandinavian runes, on both clay tiles and wooden discs. Modern authorities on this subject are springing up like mushrooms all over Europe, and each seems to have a slightly different approach to the matter!

Perhaps psychometry was the most powerful divinatory system used by the old lady, sitting by the hearth of her cottage. Today this is usually done by 'reading' an object which has belonged to the individual questioner for a while. The psychometrist takes the object in her hand and perhaps by holding it to the forehead, over the 'third eye' of psychic vision, or the brow *chakra*, that wheel of violet light, she is able to sense things from the history of the questioner, and often future developments. Like most magical systems that work, this is very simple but not necessarily easy. You can teach yourself how to do it by getting people you don't know too well to give you things to hold. Take the object and get into your relaxed and switched-off mode and immediately begin to speak of the images and feelings that come into your mind. The most vital component of this method is that you have to work fast, not allowing the logical side of your brain to interfere by trying to make neat sentences or clarify visions. Take the object, relax and speak. You may find a jumble of words, images, sensations or thoughts come to you, and it will be among this outpouring that the true, accurate and relevant material will be found. If you hesitate and try to rationalise, or explain what you are seeing or feeling, you will lose the vital flow and your reading will turn into logical guesswork!

It is well worth the effort of mastering this old art because it means that as you shake hands with a stranger, immediately you will know something about them, their motives for meeting you, how you might be able to help them, or the fact that they may cause you harm or pain. Touching a person, especially holding his hand, can open a very powerful channel of information, which of course flows in both directions. If you are able to read something about the person you are touching, he may, if he is trained or naturally sensitive, be able to assess you. This art can be applied when you are being interviewed or interviewing for a new job, meeting a friend, lover or enemy.

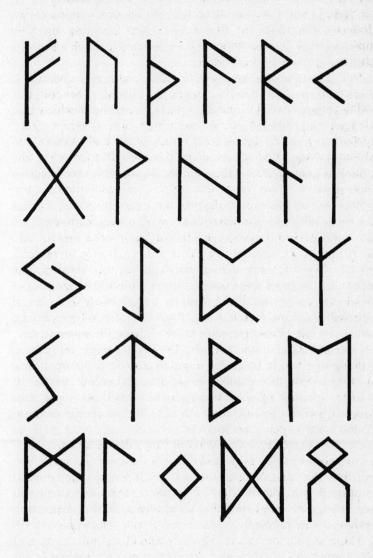

Who knows what you may learn from the brief touch of a stranger's hand, or even a kiss from a dearly beloved.

All forms of divination rely on the diviner being able to open herself to those subtle levels of communication which are all around us all the time just as radio waves are, but are undetected until we have the equipment correctly tuned to interpret the signals. Learning these arts of magic and the traditional psychic skills of the wise ones of old requires two things. The first is the ability to open our awareness up to access more information than is generally available to our five ordinary senses of sight, hearing, taste, smell and touch, so that we have 'super-hearing', 'second sight', 'ultrasensitive touch' and an 'extraordinary sense of taste/smell' which allows us to perceive things that others do not notice. The second is the ability to make sense of these subtle clues and gain knowledge from them.

The best way of explaining how these extra-sensitive abilities can be developed is by saying that we all have a sixth sense, an old concept but increasingly found true, as scientists and magicians work together in those fields where their studies overlap, in parascience, paraphysics and 'psi' experiments. The technique has been mentioned before, for it is an altered state of awareness, achieved quite simply by allowing the normal physical reactions to relax and thus the focus of our trained awareness can be redirected to other matters. This art can only be learned, like any other art, by regular practice, just as playing the violin requires regular practice. Spend a few minutes every day gaining new information by looking at Nature, reading relevant books, talking to those wiser than yourself, which may include both old folk and young children. Watch what is going on in your environment, try to read the body language of everyone you encounter, stretch your senses, always aiming to be calm and relaxed about it. Gradually you will find that you do know things beyond what your normal senses tell you, that flashes of intuition strike you when you need such guidance, and all sorts of ideas and the solutions to problems flow naturally to you.

There is no short cut to regular planned attempts at each of these old skills. We have to learn them artificially, whereas our ancestors, by the very steady and slow nature of many of their lives, were able to broaden their awareness because book learning and its strictures had very little impact in their daily round. If you think about it, we are reading most of the time, road signs, instructions on packets of things, names of shops, reference books, shopping lists and advertisements. We may not be consciously noting much of what our eyes scan, yet all of it is being recorded on some mental tape recorder, and could be played back again if absolutely necessary. Our forebears similarly recorded aspects of their unliterary lives, the words of children's games, the flowers, trees and plants in fields and gardens, the weather and any harbingers of change like wild flowers closing before rain, or flights of birds fleeing stormy weather at sea. The feel of the earth turned by the plough would mean something to the farmer and his ploughman, the temper of the horses, the rising of the bread dough, the direction of the wind, clouds on the horizon, and the colour of the sunrise. All these messages from Nature would leave us bewildered, even if we noticed them at all, yet they were the books of our ancestors, the newspapers, the weather forecast, the shapes of things to come.

We have to learn to awaken our gentle senses, our intuition and our feelings about things from which we may be unable to receive direct information. These are all aspects of divination, for the channel from the divine to the mundane is within each of us, as unregarded sense which we have neglected since childhood. Our task, as magically-minded adults, is to re-examine such skills as we used to have and bring them back under our conscious control. Like many games, most of the psychic arts need to be tackled in a playful or lighthearted manner, for nothing stops them working more than trying too hard. It is for this reason that newcomers to many of the psychic arts have immediate success, and then struggle to return to the ease and accuracy that they first achieved in some arcane experiment, like psychometry or ESP, for example. Lots of people trying to guess the colour or suit of playing cards, as a kind of psychic game, score very highly on the first run, but then fall back to nearer average later on. The same applies to many of the magical mental skills. For example, the first time you try to read Tarot cards or scry in a crystal or glass ball, you may get an amazing effect, which then deserts you. The next time you would consciously be trying harder, and that alone can prevent you being able to use your natural talents.

Today, when people are learning these ancient magical skills anew, it has been found that the more lighthearted and play-like

the attempts at reading tea leaves or at psychometry, or
the more story-like the inner journeys are, the clearer the
impressions and the greater the new knowledge gained from
these experiments may be. It does help to begin among friends,
and in a relaxed and unforced atmosphere. This is always what
is aimed at in rituals and in the way that much magical work is
approached. The best possible psychic ambience is created by a
different but hopefully pleasant atmosphere, lit by candles,
sweetly scented with incense or aromatic oils, and with a little
expectation and concentration applied within those quiet
moments. Being free from the pressure of other activities, or
unnecessary feelings of guilt brought on by the fact that you are
taking some time for yourself, away from the needs of the
family, job or society, can go a long way to releasing the
freedom of spirit which will allow that spark of divinity within
you to make itself manifest, to teach, inspire or grant you
healing. Relax, set up a quiet place, and ask for help, and it will
surely be given.

Another very old magical skill shared by witches and oracles
was that of far sight, in the witches' case normally aided by
something to stare into or at. Today this is often a glass ball,
occasionally the far more expensive rock crystal, but just as
effective and far less destructive to the crystal mountains in
America, is a bowl of water or a black-painted recycled clock
glass. It has become very fashionable to use crystals for almost
everything, from scrying (the art of crystal gazing) to
pendulums, another form of divination, and for many types of
healing. This is not to be encouraged for at least two reasons.
First, the way that crystals are collected requires blowing up
seams of rock, often deep inside crystal-lined caves. Crystals,
like coal and other minerals, are a finite resource and the
destruction of their habitat could be seen as nearly as important
as the destruction of the forests where wild plants and animals
live. Lots of money is made by unscrupulous dealers selling
'magic crystals' which have been torn from their matrices after
millions of years to be sold as trendy wand tips or pendants and
so on. If you want a crystal, yes *one* for yourself, go to a beach in
Cornwall or a Welsh mountain and find one. Take care that
you do not damage anything, for they can be found washed up by
the sea, or in rivers in the mountains. Small crystal clusters are
quite common in many forms of rock, from flint nodules, again
from some beaches, to crystalline veins in many hard rocks.

You will soon see that getting even one crystal might require hard work, but it would be of great value to you because of this. Like every aspect of practical magic, the more work you do on your own behalf, the more powerful the outcome.

Another misuse of crystals is the common underestimation of their innate power. People are always unthinkingly pointing crystals at each other, being unaware or unable to see the ray of energy which issues from the point of these beautiful stones. If the crystal has been quarried carefully its own inherent power is undamaged, and it can be used for healing by someone who is properly aware of what he is doing. In the hands of the untrained or the unwary, it can give off a nasty burst of unsettling force, so don't play with crystals. Also, don't go round planting them in sacred sites. The ancient people chose the special crystalline stones which form the vast majority of stone circles, ellipses or rows because they had special power, carefully balanced with Earth's own harmonies. Going round randomly sticking other bits of raped crystal into these areas may disrupt or change the very magical nature of these ancient monuments because modern people scarcely understand anything about this monolithic culture and its science. Take nothing but mental pictures and leave nothing but footprints, for these will be the keys to sacred sites which you can reawaken in your own meditation spot, where and when you need them.

One very simple way you can begin to explore your own link with divinity is to make a pendulum. Yes, make one. It only requires a small, symmetrical weight, a short length of some kind of thin cord or flexible string and about a quarter of an hour to start with. The best pendulums feel right in weight and length in your hand, and will swing freely in all directions. A single fixing spot at the top of the weight, or bob as it is known in the trade, will ensure an even swing both in straight lines and circles. If you use a doubled chain and some sort of pendant you will find that this set up prefers to swing in only one direction and is best avoided by beginners. A heavy bead, a proper, very small brass plumb bob, or a polished stone with a hole in it or a ring glued to it will do. Picture cord is cheap and is excellent for pendulums as it is woven instead of being twisted to stop it unravelling when your pendulum swings. I made several good dowsing pendulums with large glass marbles which had a chip off them, by glueing the burned and flattened end of the cord to the flat spot. The marbles were free from a toy shop as they had

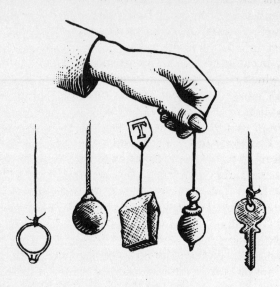

been damaged in transit, and the cord was about 20p per metre! You can pay pounds for fancy pendulums but they work no better than something you picked up for pennies, or found at the back of a drawer! Also, if you make the thing it will be closely attuned to you and work better, by the law of magic.

Get your weight and string and hold it over the top finger of a loose fist, so that the bob hangs about a stretched handspan below your hand. There are no hard and fast rules about how long or short or heavy such a pendulum may be; as you work, it will become clear what feels right to you, ultimately the only criterion in magic. Hold your other hand flat, a bit below the bob, and ask it, out loud if you like, 'Is my name .....?' stating your ordinary name. Relax and idly watch what happens to the bob, whilst forgetting about both hands. After a few moments the bob ought to be making some sort of swing. Ask it to show you more clearly, so that the circle or straight line can be determined. Then ask a few more questions to which the answer is 'Yes': the day of the week, the state of the weather, your address. All very mundane matters, but in each case the swing should be the same one of roughly four options. Pendulums can swing in clockwise or anticlockwise circles, towards and away from your body, and right/left across you. They sometimes stop, or hesitate if a question is unclear. Often it is easier to allow a slight swing to occur before you ask a question, because the subconscious movements of your hand muscles which cause it to answer will work more efficiently if they don't have to overcome inertia to begin with. Once you have established something which means 'Yes' to you and your pendulum, try some questions to which you know the answer to be 'No'. You ought to get a different swing, perhaps a line if a circle before, or the opposite direction of circle, but there should be an unmistakable difference. Try alternative questions for 'Yes' and 'No'. The movements may be slight to begin with, but as you relax and play the game, you will get stronger and faster reactions. You will find that most children can do this without any kind of hesitation, much better than some adults, and men tend to find this harder than women.

When you have established this basic code in respect of

When you have established this basic code in respect of yourself (and, after a few attempts, nine out of ten people can get This is necessary because occasionally the results reverse when you are asking questions about another person. It does help to be sure that 'Yes' is 'Yes' and 'No' is 'No' when dealing with someone else, especially if you are trying to find a proper herbal remedy to help them or checking food for allergic reactions, for which a well-trained pendulum is ideal. Check things in your own life – chemicals, soaps, foods, as well as medicines like the Bach Flower Remedies, which a pendulum will often pick out more swiftly than you could by reading the booklet. If you offer healing, it is worth asking the pendulum if you can help the patient, whether you *should* help him or her and, if you go down a list of what you have to offer, in which way you can best help that person get well.

Dowsing with a hazel or willow rod takes a bit more practice as the essential grip is quite hard to get right. The Y-shaped rod is held in both hands, with palms up, so that the ends cross the palms from the little finger side, with the tips sticking out between thumb and first finger. This tucks the elbows in and makes the wrists flex backwards, so that the whole rod is parallel to the ground. Then pull a little outwards, putting tension on the Y-joint of the rod. This is why hazel or willow woods are

used, because they will bend and not snap at this point. They are also connected with water, magically!

Walk towards a known source of water, in a bucket or hose, as this is a bit clumsy to use indoors. Running water reacts faster, so that as you cross the flow in a hose, for example, the rod will twist in your hands, usually so that the tip points down – although some people find it flies up, and can smack you on the nose, if you happen to have the 'fluence' particularly strongly! Keep at it until you get a clear reaction in the lightly gripped rod. If you clutch it too tight it will hurt your hands, raising blisters if you wear big rings and grip too hard.

There are a number of excellent books to 'teach yourself dowsing' with both the pendulum and the rod, explaining the way to locate pipes, seats of illness in humans and animals, allergies, mineral deposits, and lost treasure. Children can normally learn both methods quite fast, and 'treasure hunting' for a small coin hidden under a carpet or a toy concealed in long grass can keep them amused for hours. Like many other magical arts, if you are relaxed and have a 'let's give it a go' sort of mental attitude, rather than gritting your teeth and clenching your hands around the hazel rod or pendulum cord, you will succeed more often. It is a useful skill, in any case, for locating lost objects in your home, or a stolen car or wallet, for example, as well as helping select an appropriate remedy or herb.

In the old days the witches and Wise Ones would have a personal system of divination for telling futures for those who came to visit them. Some would scry or crystal-gaze in any dark or shiny material – even a cauldron of bubbling soup over the fire – or in the hot embers, the patterns of smoke, the flights of birds, or the shadows of leaves on the trees overhead. Today we have the hexagrams of the I Ching, the Tarot cards, the rune stones or the many varieties of divinatory images implanted on cards or plastic tablets. You can teach yourself to divine in the old way by collecting a dozen or so small objects which represent concepts like 'travel', 'good news', 'luck', 'money', 'growth', 'change', 'stability', 'love or harmony', 'quarrels or law suits', 'authority' and many other similar ideas. These could be pictures from magazines stuck to small cards, making your own mini-Tarot, or a stone for stability, a feather for travel, a postage stamp for news and so on. If you hunt around those odd corners or drawers or boxes of old birthday cards I am sure you will gain inspiration. Take your time, and also look out for a small box to keep them in. This could be decorated with felt, jewels, embroidery or stuck-on pictures, if you are feeling artistic, for it all helps link your consciousness to the symbols you have chosen. When you have as many items as you feel you will need, thinking of each object as a phrase or saying in answer to your question, hold the box between your hands, think hard about the query and silently, if you like, ask that the Spirit of Divination help you see the answer. Then shoot the objects loosely along the floor, or onto a table. Look at the relationships; those closest to you will speak loudest and soonest, those further away will be later developments. Any that fall to the floor or are hidden by other objects, or fall 'face down' if that is possible, should be ignored. You may be amazed how deep the answers from such a primitive and personal system can be. Do try it. It is much easier to learn with than someone else's ideas developed into their Tarot, or new I Ching.

Another old method, which is really a development of the object oracle, is the use of short sticks deliberately cut from trees. In the days of the Druid priests this was a very important divination system. Short rods of about twenty native trees were carefully collected, and the diviner, knowing the uses and magical connections of every sort of tree, could throw down the bundle, after making a prayer for guidance, and the divinity would answer, again through the positions and interlacing of the various sticks. If you have the patience you can make a

simplified version of this for yourself. I hope no one tries to
make sets to sell, because these would harm trees and have very
little value to the buyer.

You will need to cut just one small branch from each of your
chosen trees, so you will need some sharp secateurs, as it is best
to take only twigs about as thick as your middle finger and
about a handspan long, as that was the traditional size and it
works well. If you take a sharp knife to trim off any side shoots,
you can also cut a flat surface at or towards one end of each stick
and put a number, letter or identifying mark on each one so
that you know what it is, when you have a handful. Twigs can
look extremely similar! Later on you will need to make a
cylindrical container, or find a nice box in which to keep your
magical twigs. You may also like to acquire and paint or
embroider a special cloth onto which the twigs may be shaken
or scattered when you divine with them. It is possible that in
early times this cloth had the figures of the zodiac or the twelve
houses marked upon it, so that a kind of instant tree horoscope
would be produced. There is very little recorded information
about this Celtic form of divination, and some recent books on
the matter seem to be largely guesswork, but if you venture into
the past, through far memory, you may be able to see clearly
how it was done.

The trees suggested below are some of the traditional ones,
with meanings from which you can elaborate your own system.
In some cases I have suggested 'a fruit tree' rather than apple or
cherry, for example, as you may not always have access to every
kind of tree. Whatever you do, take your time. My own
collection of about thirty trees, some native, some introduced,
took about two years to gather, taking only one twig from any
species, and having to travel across the country as certain kinds
of trees just don't grow in the vicinity. There are 'introduced'
species of tree in this list as they represent the new ideas,
technologies and activities which simply did not exist in the
Druids' age. A basic set of thirteen trees would include oak,
ash, willow, rowan, sycamore, holly, yew, hawthorn (may),
horse-chestnut, elder, as well as a fruit tree (ideally apple), a
hedge tree like privet or laurel, and a conifer, fir or pine.
Because these trees are being used symbolically, some have
shared meanings; the apple, for example, is held both as a
Tree of Life and of Wisdom. In the Celtic tradition a branch of
flowering apple was a safe passport from this world to the

Otherworld and, more importantly, a passport for a safe return. Pear or cherry does not have the same meaning, but trees should not be cut when they are flowering in any case. Six of these trees are linked traditionally with the Goddess, and six can be tools of the God. The thirteenth, the horse-chestnut, a fairly recent introduction to Britain, is symbolic of children, partly because of its association with the game of conkers. Although, like most Goddess trees, it has white flowers, its wood has many practical uses, linking it with craftsmen gods.

OAK:
This is a God tree, symbolising authority, strength, endurance and earthly power, also plenty. A Midsummer tree, sometimes.

ASH:
A God tree of kingship, craftsmanship – as tool handles were usually made of ash staffs – protection on journeys, guidance in practical matters. The Norse Tree of Knowledge from which Odin gained the runes.

ROWAN OR MOUNTAIN ASH:
A Goddess tree, used to ward off harm, both magically and practically. A good stick for a natural magician's wand. It has white flowers and red berries – both Goddess colours.

APPLE (OR A FRUIT TREE):
This is again a Goddess tree, as most fruit trees have white or pink flowers, but apple is especially magical. It represents a gaining of knowledge and wisdom, it is the tree which outlives death, and inside the sacred fruit there is a magical sign of Light and Hope. Apple protects the bearer as he travels through the worlds, and awakens insight and magical power.

SYCAMORE:
A God tree, used by carvers of love-spoons as a symbol of offered or received love, and of hard work, craftsmanship and care. It is a spring tree, first to leaf, and is also often that from which Jack-in-the-Green peers forth.

HOLLY:
A God tree, symbol of sacrifice and life reborn for it is an evergreen. A winter tree, closely associated with the Yule feast. It shows that sacrifices made will be repaid threefold.

YEW:
Goddess tree, symbol of eternal life, death and rebirth. Be careful cutting this one for its leaves are poisonous to animals and people, and though

birds may eat its sweet red seeds with impunity, humans are poisoned by them. This stands for changes in the pattern of things, old age, stability in the long term and patience.

HORSE-CHESTNUT: A child's tree, games, sport, youth and folly. The spring symbol, full of promise and life. It also represents journeys, for the horse was the oldest form of transport. It is the smith's tree, and he was master of the magic of making things, creativity and invention. Look up Wayland Smith!

HAWTHORN (OR MAY): This is a Goddess tree of protection, for quickthorn was often used for hedges and also its flowering marked the beginning of summer. It is the Maiden's tree, sacred lover and playmate, joy and fun above other things. Surprise gifts or outings may appear.

ELDER: Another Goddess tree with white summer flowers and black autumn fruit, ideal for the dark ritual wine. She is the Goddess in the dark part of the year, from Hallowe'en to Yule, bringer of gifts of the spirit, prophecy and visions. Revelations spring from her appearance in a reading.

WILLOW: Another Goddess tree, this time of healing, both of the body (aspirin is derived originally from willow trees) and of the soul. This can mean the uncovering of the roots of a problem and the cleansing of the spirit, perhaps by a good cry! Just as the besom, made of birch twigs, ash handle and willow bindings, cleared the circle, so the willow brightens the view of the future.

PINE (OR ANY OTHER CONIFER): A God tree, sweet-scented, with sharp evergreen needles (except larch, which is bare in winter), used to build boats for travel, or houses for protection, or furniture for comfort. Its woodsmoke offers prayers a ride to heaven, so wishes may be granted, if they are spoken truly.

LAUREL (OR ANY HEDGE PLANT): This is a symbol of divine protection, law, an edge or barrier to something. Often you will have a hunch about how a judgement will go, or how you can bring a long-running dispute to an end. It will help you focus on what is really the crux of the matter, and limit your wasted time and effort.

This list and the associations with each tree are very basic, because to make any system of divination work for you, you need to find symbols and ideas which you associate with every card, stick or tree. You will need to spend time sorting out the ideas about each tree while you are collecting, refining and allowing each twig to dry. Unless you happen to have an arboretum at the bottom of your garden, or know someone who works at Kew Gardens, you are going to have to search around your home area, be it city or countryside, to locate every tree on the list you should make.

When the twigs have all been gathered, and allowed to dry in an upright position to keep them straight, you can cut a slice off the 'bottom' end and mark it with a rune or identifying mark of your own so that you don't forget what it is. You can round the ends of the twigs with a piece of sandpaper, but it is best to leave the bark and any rough places or small twig junctions as Nature intended. Each will give that twig a character which will help with future readings.

To divine, you will need to have discovered something about the symbolism of each tree for yourself, and have learned how to identify each quickly as it lies before you. The Druids apparently shook the container three times so that a few twigs fell out onto their special cloth, and then they read these for answers to the question, which they thought about as they shook the box. The twigs can be considered in all sorts of ways, but I use the following simple method. Distance from you equals time, so that those twigs further away will mean something will happen later than those closest. Twigs touching or crossing each other have to be read together. Tops away from you are positive symbols whereas the marked 'bottoms' mean delays or problems in whatever they individually symbolise. The twigs which didn't fall out (and some should always be left in the box or tube) have no relevance to the particular question. Obviously, certain trees may represent certain people or jobs, some trees may seem to you lucky or unlucky, some suggest growth, fruition of plans, travel or communications, perhaps, some dealings with authority or the law or older people or children. You must sort this out for yourself, partly by research into the uses of various woods, and by meditating upon your own twig, thinking about the nature of the tree it was cut from, where it grew and so on. Get a small book and use one page for each tree, adding in all the new ideas you have until every single twig has a clear and complex message for you. Look at each alone, and then with other twigs. Look at the shapes they form: are these runes, or patterns you can read like tea leaves? Although it is simple, this can be a very effective and wide-ranging divination system.

Exercises

Like most of the real arts of the village witches, dowsing and divination are really very simple. Modern folk try to make them more complicated because we are complicated people, and seem to need to make things hard for ourselves. Play at dowsing with a twig or pendulum and you can surprise yourself with the results you achieve; try to use 'scientific' explanations for such powers, or 'work at them' with gritted teeth, and you will fail. If you do fail at any of these tasks, take that as a valuable lesson and try again. You wouldn't expect to play the violin after one go, would you? Magic is the same. It is an art and a knack, gained by trying gently.

There are lots of basic exercises in the chapter for your eighth moon of work. Try psychometry and pendulum dowsing, and later on, when you have gained some confidence from your natural abilities to do those to some extent, go out and cut yourself a dowsing rod from a hazel or willow tree. Mastering rod dowsing is harder because the grip is difficult to describe and feels very unnatural, but it does work for most people who persevere.

Try a pendulum at your local sacred site. See how it reacts and then ask it why. With any sort of divination it is asking the right questions which produces the most effective answers. Each system has a limited 'language' of expressions; a pendulum can only say 'Yes' or 'No', remember, so can't make comparisons. The Tarot can tell you 78 things, multiplied by however many cards you draw. You will have to learn to ask things in a way which ensures a proper and coherent answer.

Have a go at scrying with any dark glass or bowl of water set on a black cloth, by candle light. Try until you succeed.

Sort out a selection of omen objects for your own personal divination set. Use them and broaden your awareness, whilst very relaxed, to seek answers to questions about travel or communication from friends, about your magical progress and

how you can make closer contact with the Old Ones. You may
well be surprised at the clarity of the answers such 'primitive'
systems give you. Allow your own inner voice to expand what
the symbols alone indicate, for that is the true art of divination,
or divine inspiration.

Carefully make a set of the Tree Oracle, and a container for
it, if that attracts you. Otherwise get a set of runes or Tarot
cards and really begin to learn what they can say to you,
studying one symbol at a time. Always record in your Book of
Illumination anything which you learn, the question and
answers or symbols of the response, and your own expanded
reading of it.

Again, here are just a few books – there are various systems
of divination, ancient and modern, and you will need to use
your growing powers of discretion to select ones which will help
you on your quest for ancient knowledge.

Tom Graves, *Dowsing: Techniques and Applications* (Turnstone)
Tom Graves, *The Elements of Pendulum Dowsing* (Element
Books)
Liz and Colin Murray, *The Celtic Tree Oracle* (divination
system) (Century)
Tony Willis, *The Runic Workbook* (Aquarian)
Tony Willis, *Magick and the Tarot* (Aquarian)
Caitlín and John Matthews, *The Arthurian Tarot* (Aquarian)
Marian Green, *The Path Through the Labyrinth* (Element Books)

9.

PLANT POWER

The realm of plants provides everything our body needs for a balanced and integrated existence. However, we are more than just a body; we also have consciousness, which brings other factors onto the stage. We not only have to take our animal body into consideration, but also our mind, our emotions and our spiritual nature. Harmony is no longer simply a matter of right diet or even right herbs, but also a matter of right feelings, right thoughts, lifestyle, actions, attunement – harmony of right relationship to our world . . .

David Hoffman: *The Holistic Herbal*

Witches have nearly always had a sinister reputation which, on the whole, they have not deserved. In earlier times their knowledge of healing, psychological counselling, far-seeing and veterinary medicine was unrivalled in country districts. Often the Wise Woman was also the midwife and probably it was also she who laid out the dead before their burial. So, she had knowledge of bringing forth into life, and of saying a respectful farewell to the departed. Her healing arts would have been shared certainly by the Cunning Man, who rather than dealing with childbirth in people, was probably the expert with animals, helping calves and foals and lambs into the world. His skill with cattle and horses would be similar to that skill attributed to the gypsies, even in the modern world, in that he could control wild-natured bulls or unbroken stallions just by a look, or the use of the horseman's secret word, or traditional scents which calm a savage beast.

Because of their shared knowledge of herbs, some of which heal and some of which can bring sleep or trance or death, they would have been feared. It was this fear in the common people, and sometimes a feeling of envy among the Church fathers in the Middle Ages, in whose power normally rested the skills of healing and magical techniques, that was the cause of distrust from the Church, which eventually led to persecution.

When many of the modern drugs were known only in their potent herbal forms such knowledge was power, and it might often have been the case that if a severely ill or injured person could not be helped he would receive a dose of one of the deadly extracts from a poisonous plant, and gain rest in that way. If the Wise Woman were able to assist newborn babies safely into the world, even sometimes at the cost of the mother's life, and ease the passing of the old or dying, so they held sway over both ends of human existence, but the Church saw this function as one for their God alone. However, the common folk would more readily have turned to the local bonesetter to have their dislocations or broken bones aligned and splinted, than see what the monks or nuns could do.

Much of the ancient plant lore is being re-examined as a result of fears about losses of tree cover, not only in the Amazon jungles, but in parts of Europe, America and Australia. Those people who lived in harmony with the plants would be well aware of their special properties, to heal, to bring visions, to flavour food, to provide raw materials for making rope or clothes or shelter. They would know which would provide coloured dyestuffs; or clean septic wounds or animal bites; which would ward off flying insects or moths from clothes or freshen the atmosphere inside their homes. Some were simply nourishing for the body, others fed the spirit or awakened inner visions, some brought a swift and painless death, an easier childbirth, deep sleep or enhanced wakefulness, just as many modern drugs can do. Natural herbal preparations, however, often produce the desired result without any of the harmful side-effects so prevalent with modern pharmaceuticals.

It is not possible to look at the whole matter of traditional herbal medicine here, nor is it wise to start playing about with medicinal plants without receiving proper training first. Certainly you can grow a few herbs for the pot, learn to make natural fruit and flower wines, and use scented oils in small doses to perfume your room or bath, or as massage oils, so long are you are careful. But beyond that you do need proper instruction, and not just a weekend class on 'Herbalism for the Town Dweller'. Do get yourself some good illustrated books on common trees, plants and herbs, and go out and learn to recognise every growing thing, in summer and in winter. Smell the flowers, bark, leaves and sap of various culinary plants, garden flowers and weeds, so that if you take up the study of herbal medicine seriously you will quickly be able to recognise exactly which plant you are dealing with. There are many similar-looking plants to be found in the countryside; some are harmless and look decorative in the house, others can be deadly and a drop of juice in a cut, or a carelessly licked lip onto which some sap may have been splattered can have serious consequences. Please be very careful if you have young children or feckless adults with you when you go on a plant-hunting expedition, especially if you decide to collect a few nice mushrooms for the pot!

One of the simplest and safest forms of plant lore, traditional to our culture, is the use of herbal teas, which can assist with minor complaints and has the added advantage of aiding some of the psychic aspects of your life too. By awakening your perceptions you will be able to apply whatever therapies you aim to master more effectively or, when your common sense or the Goddess tells you, abstain from offering help in certain instances. Any health food shop will have a range of teas made with properly prepared natural herbs. To begin with, start with single plants in tea bags, if you are unsure as to their effects, or as loose herbs from a herbalist, which are much cheaper. Chamomile, nettle, comfrey, lemon balm, rosehip and peppermint are good ones to start with, as each has a fairly obvious effect, and most can be used on common complaints.

It may be worth looking out for a tea infuser, which is a metal net or perforated sphere in which about a teaspoon per person of the dried herb is placed, and which is then immersed in freshly boiled water for three to five minutes. You can simply put a teaspoon of loose herbs into a china, pottery or glass mug or jug and then strain the infusion into another cup after a few minutes, if you prefer. You may find some of these herbs have unfamiliar tastes, and so the addition of a little clear honey or even a squeeze of lemon juice might make them more palatable. You will usually find that herbs need longer to steep than ordinary tea, as the essential oils which give out the flavour and effects are slower to come out than those in tea.

The sorts of complaints the above-mentioned herbs can help with include anxiety and indigestion (chamomile and/or peppermint); tiredness, especially during a cold or after winter (rosehip or nettle). Lemon balm is useful in cases of nervous reactions, stress and upset stomach complaints, and it will ease anxiety. Comfrey tea can help with coughs or bronchitis, and it may be applied to cuts and bruises. You may well find that a cup of chamomile tea, perhaps flavoured with lemon balm, will help you to relax and meditate, and in that state gain insight into other suitable treatments for patients or friends, or to assist your own health. Do be very careful that you know what you are doing and use only the stated dose of any herb. If in doubt, ask for time to consult your books or your inner self, or the Goddess of Healing.

There are many excellent books on basic herbal medicine, with clear descriptions of healing plants, their uses and manner of collection, so study these properly and, if you can, get some personal tuition in the recognition of plants and how to cultivate or collect them for medicine. Often there are local evening classes in the uses of plants, for healing, dyes, cooking and so on and this can be an excellent introduction to the subject. There are also a number of schools of herbal medicine which run personal and postal courses of tuition, many leading you into contact with like-minded souls who may share your interest in other aspects of occult work, magic or witchcraft.

Because plants, in all their forms, played such an important part in the work of the Old Wise Ones, and because today people are becoming increasingly aware of the importance of using natural things as far as possible, there is a wide variety of subjects which any neo-witch or modern shaman ought to have a go at. If you think about it, mankind has found a use for trees, shrubs, herbs, plants, fungi, mosses, bulbs and corms. We also use every part of every plant for something, if only making compost! Often we eat the seeds, fruits, berries, nuts or leaves, we may use the bark for dye, or a medicine, or to make something. Some shrubs produce scented gums, and resins are extracted for use as incense, in paint and to scent a room. Flowers may be used simply as decorations but they may also be dried, pressed and made into cards for celebrations, or they may be blended to make pot-pourri. Some can be eaten, as can seaweeds, watercress and the 'fiddleheads' of uncurling bracken. Many tubers, like potatoes, are staple foods, and all the onion family, including garlic, have beneficial antiseptic properties. Even humble grasses can be woven into mats or twined into baskets.

Wines can be made from all fruits, some vegetables and lots
of flowers, including many considered as weeds. Many wild
plants, like elder or blackberries, yield wonderful wines, ideal
for drinking at feasts. The basic ingredients can be collected one
year, with dandelions available around Beltane at the beginning
of May, for instance, which when made into wine and matured
will be ready to drink the next year. Midsummer sees vast
amounts of white, sweetly-scented elder blossom on many a
field hedge, and this can be turned into elder champagne, a
heady, fragrant sparkling white wine, to be followed by the very
dark red elderberry wine made later in the year. Parsnips,
gooseberries, strawberries, apples and oranges can all be turned
into delightful wines, if you happen to have a glut in the garden,
or be able to lay your hands on a supply from a friendly fruit
shop. Apples or pears can be made into cider or perry even if
they are a bit bruised, as they have to be crushed first.

Most towns now seem to have 'brew it yourself' shops or
large branches of chemists which have a homemade wine and
beer section where the basic equipment can be bought, along
with suitable yeasts, or hops if you prefer beer or lager. There
are kits which can teach you the methods without the effort of
collecting or preparing the raw fruits, and this may be sufficient
to get you interested. Once you have gained confidence in the
end result, you will have a cheap supply of special wines for
your feasts, or for presents to your friends. Most libraries have
large sections of books on home winemaking or beer-brewing,
and ways of turning the most unlikely things into sweet or dry
drinks. If you don't drink alcohol, and some modern pagans
don't, then you can make cordials from fruits or non-alcoholic
punches, crushes and syrups. If you keep bees or know anyone
who does, or can get hold of some good honey in quantity, you
can make that magical and ancient sacred drink of the Celts,
mead. The better and more aromatic the honey the better the
mead, and if you can let it mature for a year or five, you will
end up with a wonderful dry golden beverage which is fit for the
gods.

Honey is also a traditional additive in many old incense
blends, and again herbs and spices, like lavender, rosemary,
bay, wormwood, sage, cinnamon or cloves, can be part of your
own special blends. Although the Church used to use things like
frankincense or myrrh in their services, and many churches still
do (monasteries providing useful supplies of the required gums

and resins to pagans and Christians alike) it is worth experimenting a bit with what you can collect for yourself. Try each substance on its own on a small part of a lighted charcoal block – you can get the sort designed for burning incense from most of the occult suppliers, church shops or esoteric mail order companies. Don't try burning incense on barbeque charcoal, it won't light properly indoors. You can collect a few basic incenses from suppliers, too, but try the single gums first.

Some trees found in Britain will ooze resins if they have been cut and you can chip off small pieces, often mixed with tree bark from pine, larch and other conifers. Apple wood may be resinous but dried and burned it smells sweet, and cherry and plum trees give out gum too. Most culinary herbs will burn, but if you use the dried stems rather than the leaves you will get better results. Any good herbal book will tell you which plants can be used either for relaxation or to awaken your inner psychic powers. Most of the traditional temple incenses contained a mixture of sweet and aromatic gums and resins which had a consciousness-raising effect.

Nowadays people perfume their homes by using oil burners or vaporisers with scented oils, but some of these are made from artificial essences and so may not have the same effects as the pure rose or jasmine flowers, for example. Try to find out what the sources of such aromatics are because the fake ones will do no good to your psychic powers, and may have unpleasant side-effects. The price is a good indicator, for even common ones like rose can cost a great deal for the pure essence. You can make lavender or pine oil yourself, quite easily, by getting some light vegetable oil, sunflower or almond, and putting dried lavender heads or resinous chips of pine wood into them. If you happen to be near a wooden boat yard when they are repairing a vessel with larch or pitchpine you may be able to collect some wonderful smelly shavings. The balsam poplar has a superb scent in about late April or early May when its small sticky buds are breaking open. To me, this is one of the most glorious scents in nature. The brown, sticky bud covers can be collected and stored in a dry jar for use in incense or pot-pourri.

Many herbs are most commonly used to flavour food, and again there are plenty of excellent books on the subject. You can grow a vast range of edible plants in Britain today, but many of these used to be picked in the wild, in the good old unpolluted days of the horse and cart! Flowers were added to many dishes and salads, partly for decoration, and because they are known to contain valuable minerals and vitamins. If you do happen to find nasturtiums or rose petals on your plate, do eat them, they taste nice and are good for you. Learn a bit about making garlands out of twining plants, with bright seasonal flowers woven in to decorate your altar staff, if you go in for using the older method of making a place sacred. You can wear a chaplet of flowers around your head, or a necklace of leaves and brightly coloured seed heads, to celebrate the full moon or the harvest feast. Learn to set up a bowl of special flowers or growing plants as each season changes, or to mark the moons or your own personal anniversaries, men as well as women, for this was one of the priestly tasks of the Ancient Mysteries. If you are unable to set aside a room for magic and have no garden, then a tiny indoor shrine, with sea shells, plants, dried branches or even a mini herb garden will be accepted by the Goddess of Earth as a suitable offering.

If you happen to be artistic and wish to add some of the old crafts to your repertoire, another ancient magic was that of dyeing, using natural plant colours and various chemical mordants to fix the colours. Material made from natural fibres can be dyed in that way, unless you also wish to learn to spin wool and dye that. A wide range of soft countryside colours can be produced from old plants, like blue from woad or greeny-yellow from goldenrod. Again, many weeds have a use in dyeing, producing muted reds, greens, yellows, russets, browns and blues. You seldom get the bright artificial colours made from chemical dyes but there is a charm and naturalness found in those faded-looking hues which Nature herself provides. You might simply be able to find plant-dyed material to make a robe, or wool to knit a magical scarf or stole from, especially if you visit craft fairs.

Another application which is a bit less time- and space-consuming is the use of flowers, pressed and dried, to make talismans. It is a very old tradition, using the language of flowers, some for love, some meaning friendship, some showing distrust or longing, set out on a card in a pattern which turns the picture into a charm. Again, you will find excellent books on the meanings of various flowers, and how they may be preserved so that their colours and petals look lifelike. In the old days much simpler charms were made by threading certain leaves or flowers onto a twig to spell out a message, which could be hidden up a tree, or placed on your beloved's doorstep at midnight, depending on what outcome was desired. Fruit, nuts and flowers were all used to send messages, not always directly to the recipient, but magically to draw their attention to what was needed. Some mixtures would indicate a healing charm, some a spell to ward off undesired attentions or bad luck. Remember, even today we still touch wood to draw the attention of Pan, the woodland God, to our hope for success! Or we simply 'knock on wood' for luck, asking that the powers of Nature take care of us.

As you will have seen in the previous chapter, different woods could spell out messages from the future, as a very old form of divination. In the same way, dried leaves of those trees could be carefully stuck to cards and covered with transparent film, to make a kind of tree Tarot. Rubbings of the bark or thin slices of wood could be used as other forms of 'Rune sticks'. You will soon find that there is a mass of ancient lore about the uses, meanings and values of trees, their associations with particular gods or events or times of year. Don't swallow every word on 'ancient tree calendars' you may come across as gospel (oaks?)! There is little evidence that such a system existed, but certainly different woods would have been used at specific times of year, when they were most fit for the purpose in hand.

Many of the ordinary herbs and sweet-scented flowers can be easily used to scent your bath water, and are a lot cheaper and more ecologically sound than chemical bath foams. Tie some crushed herbs or flowers in a soft cloth under the tap as the water runs into the bath and this will scent the water. Lemon balm, lavender, rose petals, mint, thyme or sage are all excellent. Some dried herbs could be steeped in boiling water, and then this liquid strained into the bath. Herbs used in this way are relaxing and also some have a psychically cleansing property, so that the bath becomes the first stage in any ritual, when you will arise refreshed and ready to begin your working. You can make perfumed oil by pressing as many green herbs or flowers as possible into a jar of almond or sunflower oil, and leaving it for several days. Strain this liquid into a clean dark glass bottle and see if the scent has been transferred. If the scent is weak, put it back into a jar with a new supply of flowers or leaves, and repeat until you have a suitable aroma.

Many herbs have been used as cosmetics, particularly in shampoos, and washes made from rosemary for dark-haired people or chamomile for lighter hair can be used as the first rinsing water, after the shampoo has been washed away. Facial scrubs can be made with crushed oats and honey, and cooling lotions made from lemon balm, marigolds or goosegrass can help with chapped skin or mild sunburn. Marigold (calendula) made into an ointment is excellent after gardening or when your hands have got rough and dry. Again, you will find some very helpful books on the many applications of herbs and plants in cosmetics, cookery and winemaking in the library, or a decent-sized bookshop.

Trees and plants are attributed to the various planets, and old herbalists would prescribe treatments which assisted the position of the planets in the patient's horoscope, not just to counteract the symptoms they were suffering from. This may well be the forerunner of the increasingly popular therapy, homoeopathy, where minute doses of often quite poisonous plants and minerals are given to produce a healing reaction in the patient. For example, a plant which makes a healthy person feverish might be used to bring down the fever of a sick one. It is a very delicate and complex yet increasingly successful form of treatment used, among other well-known people, by the Royal family, who are extremely healthy and long-lived! A homoeopath asks the potential patient many strange questions and so builds up a complete picture of his or her likes and dislikes, symptoms and reactions, and then decides upon a specific homoeopathic drug, vastly diluted, which will usually clear up most conditions that person may suffer from. They do not have 'cold cures' or 'headache medicine' as such, but preparations which in a given patient will indeed shorten the effects of a cold, or ease a tension headache. Homoeopathy is especially good for migraines and all those odd illnesses and discomforts which conventional medicine has no answer to.

Learning which plants and trees and flowers are associated with which planet will help you to blend particular incenses, make flower talismans or posies to aid healing, for example, as this is a disguised way of bringing certain influences into the life of a patient who would be upset by the idea of actual 'magic'. (So long as they have asked for help in some way first!) You will also be able to add the planetary influences of trees to the list of things with which any tree is linked, when you build up your tree divination set. *Culpeper's Herbal*, still in print after many centuries, gives the old associations of plants and planets, but the more informative *Modern Herbal* by Mrs Grieve contains the whole of Culpeper plus heaps more information on pretty well every healing or useful plant, tree, herb, grass, flower, spice or growing thing you could ever want. A well-illustrated herbal book with clear drawings or photographs, especially produced for your home country, should be on the shelves of every New Age witch or pagan healer. If you can devote a section of your garden or window box to herbs you will gain the joy of seeing them grow and flower and seed at first hand.

One of the most powerful magical acts you can experience is a unity with Nature herself. This can be tested beneath the canopy of a large individual tree which, if you allow it, can become your personal counsellor and friend, or deep inside a wood, even a small one, or if there are no woodlands in your area, out along the edges of fields or rivers. Under a tree you need to sit and perform one of the relaxation exercises, completely detaching yourself from the ordinary world. You will soon feel that the tree spreads a circle of protection about itself and you, for this is the area covered by its canopy and its roots. It is an original place of power. You will be almost invisible if you sit still and allow your awareness to merge with that of the tree. Feel the upward flows of Earth energy, dark and slow like wild honey, filling the whole trunk, branches and leaves with solidity and endurance. Draw upon that force for yourself, becoming slow and heavy and patient. Then sense the down-falling rain of sky power, like a shower of tiny droplets of light, bringing vitality and a lightness of spirit. Breathe deeply, scenting the earthiness of the tree and the land which is its base, smell the leaves and twigs, and the aura of life energy around it. If you reach out with your speedy human senses you will soon detect those emanations from any tree.

This same exercise can be tried within a wood, for there you will also sense the shared tree spirit, or dryad, of the whole wood, a vast, lofty, almost invisible yet sentient being, which can offer healing for the body, mind and spirit. Such dryads will occasionally give you a small token to take home. It may only seem to be a twig which stuck into you as you sat down among the roots, or an acorn or seed pod, or just a leaf you found in your hair, but it is a key to that aspect of Nature's living family with which you need to attune yourself to make the best use of her wide variety of powers and information systems, gleaned with the heart rather than the head.

By a river you will sense two flows, one with the current, washing outwards like the human lungs exhaling stale air, and with that flow you can cast away care and the burdens of illness, worry or pain. The other is an inner sense of power connecting all waters around the earth. Pick a stem of grass or the leaf from a water plant, and holding it flat on your palms, mentally beam into it all your woes and bad feelings. Fill it with them until you can detect the weight of them pressing your hands down into your lap. Then stand up and throw the leaf into the water and watch what happens. If it swiftly drifts away with the current, vanishing from your sight, so will your worries vanish within a very short time. If it whirls around in an eddy you will need to do more work on understanding the reasons for your unhappiness, seeking, through meditation or ordinary thought, the real root cause and dealing with that yourself, with your divine powers. If the leaf sinks, then you are worrying needlessly, even if you feel something is your fault; as the wise Chinese oracle of the I Ching often says, 'There is no blame!' so you must cease fretting. If the leaf drifts back towards you, then the problem is yours and it is bigger than you imagined. Again there is an underlying cause to be found by hard work, real effort and perhaps consultation with other people who may be part of the problem. It is karmically up to you to sort it out.

A field hedge can offer similar lines of oracular information, by the movements of animals or insects towards or away from you, or the whispering voice of the wind in the leaves and grasses, the hum of bees. All these simple aspects of Nature are her voices, but we have forgotten how to listen in silence, and seek the simplicity to heal us or teach us. We expect magic to be complicated, ritualistic and intellectual, when really it is so simple, so trivial and a matter of allowing the untaught heart to speak in silence, and the unfocused attention to show us answers which have been there under our feet all the time. We won't look at these unwritten, ancient sources of wisdom because we will not acknowledge they even exist. Learn to be quiet, be still. Listen, listen, there is the voice of the Old Ones!

Exercises

As this chapter is mainly concerned with the use of plants it will be obvious that one aspect of your work as a trainee witch will

be to grow and understand the uses of as many plants and herbs
as you can. If, however, you do not have control of a garden or
even a window box, then you will have to look at the other
magical applications of herbs, trees, gums and plant products
within the occult sphere, and try them instead. Do look through
this chapter of ideas for your ninth moon of practical work and
see what you can manage, perhaps borrowing space in a
friend's garden, or cultivating an area not previously
considered suitable for plants. Even a tiny plot or collection of
containers and tubs can grow dozens of herbs, fruit trees, vines,
scented flowers and colourful foliage.

In your Book of Illumination discover suitable seasonal
plants which can be used at each of the festivals, within the
house, or as garlands for your staff. You could choose vegetarian dishes or salads as ways of celebrating the change of
seasons, which could be shared with pagan and orthodox
friends alike.

Go to a herbalist and discover which dried plants can solve
some non-medicinal problem; for example, tansy helps to keep
away flies, and horsetail can be used to polish pewter plates.

Have a go at making some drinks, even if it is from a
wine-making kit, or just special blends of fresh fruit juices.

Sniff through the culinary herbs and spices and see which might
be useful in incenses. Mrs Grieve's *Herbal* tells which planet each is
attributed to, and so can be used for blessing a talisman. Cinnamon
sticks, cloves, ginger and rosemary can be added to more
conventional incense resin mixes for interesting scents.

Make a list of all the common poisonous plants which are to
be found in gardens and hedgerows, near water or in woods.
You may be surprised how many there are.

Dry and press some flowers or leaves to make a collage in
honour of the Goddess of Nature or the Green Man.

Go at least to a 'pick your own' fruit farm and gather soft
fruit or berries, or better still, walk in the country and gather
some of the wild plants, flowers and fruits if possible. (Be aware
that many plants are protected by law and may not be dug up or
harmed.)

Find some pine or other resinous trees and collect the gum to
try in incenses.

Go and try the tree meditation several times with different
trees, and look for dryads and the aura which surrounds every
living tree.

Try the banishing spell, to get rid of a worry into running water.

Spend as much time as you can watching the sunshine on gardens, and moonlight on woods. Get to feel at home there; perhaps discover a small totem animal which can bring you messages from the Otherworld.

Look out for these books, and any others about uses of plant materials, the stories of trees and their uses.

Mrs Grieve, *A Modern Herbal* (Dover or Penguin) (This is a must!)
Edmund Launert, *Edible and Medicinal Plants* (Illustrated) (Hamilton Books)
David Hoffman, *The Holistic Herbal* (Element Books)

Do go out there and get to know some trees. They have ways of instructing us in the Old Ways, their presence is amazingly calming and energising, and knowledge of them was at the roots of much Old Wisdom.

10.

MOON MAGIC AND SOLAR CYCLES

The Moon holds a special place in magickal lore. She is the only astral body which encircles the Earth; the planets proper orbit the Sun, while the Sun itself orbits the Galactic Centre. There is thus an especially intimate relationship built up between the Moon and the Earth. The occult teaching is that the Moon acts as the transmitter for all the other planetary forces, receiving their several influences and relaying them to our planet.

Tony Willis: *Magick and the Tarot*

The power of the sun and the moon have always been considered potent influences on the activities of mankind. Today we have all sorts of scientific explanations as to the effect of sunlight on plants, or of the moon's position and the state of the tides of the sea, but to our ancestors there was a great deal more to these Lights in the Sky, and the effects they had on the world below. On one hand, both the sun and the moon were seen as being either gods and goddesses actually flying through the heavens, or, more frequently, as symbols of such luminous deities. The Druids had a concept of the Son behind the Sun, a great power hidden by the sheer brilliance of sunlight. They did not worship the actual star, which we now know forms the central axle of our solar system, but the energy, the force that great light represented.

This is the most important aspect of all magical arts. What every spell, ritual or practical working is doing is manipulating the power which is so often referred to as the Light. Today we understand that light itself is energy, transformed from fuel by heat, as in a candle flame, or by making a thin filament incandescent as in an electric bulb, but there is an inner meaning to the concept of light. This also turns up in many religions; for example, Jesus is called 'The Light of the World'

and angels are described as 'The Shining Ones'. But there is
more to it than a philosophical argument about the meaning of
words. We may see the Moon Goddess in her guise as the moon
in the sky, in one other of her phases; we may comprehend and
worship a Sun God, especially at sunrise or midsummer, but
beneath that ritual act there should be an awareness of a greater
idea. Light is a symbol of growth, it is eternal, for the light of
the first spark is still travelling outwards through the universe,
at the speed of light. It is a symbol of illumination, of 'seeing the
light' or receiving a 'flash of inspiration'. We seek
'enlightenment' which means more than simply driving out
darkness from our rooms after nightfall.

Lights in the sky, by day or night, have always attracted the
attention of the curious and though today we may scoff at the
idea of the actual planets having any possible influence on our
lives, because they are so far away, we still may consult our
horoscopes before making an important decision, or just look at
the 'Stars' in the newspaper for the day's predictions. Again
scientists, who scoffed harder than most, have begun to discover
statistical correlations between the positions of certain planets in
a person's horoscope and his skill as a writer or athlete, for
instance. Michel Gauqueline has written several books based on
such evidence, and he started out extremely sceptical about the
value of astrology.

The earliest calendars, some dating back to the Stone Age
carved on the walls of caves, seem to represent the phases of the
moon. There is a fascinating relief carving of a fat, female
goddess figure holding up a curved horn or moon-shaped object
marked into segments, perhaps indicating the days of change
from new moon to full. Pieces of deer antler have been similarly
marked by very ancient and supposedly primitive people.
Many of the earliest constructions on a grand scale of human
endeavour, the vast earthworks, the rings and ellipses of
standing stones, the long avenues, the great mile-long dikes,
seem to point to alignments of the rising or setting sun, or
moon. Stonehenge, through all the hundreds of years of its
construction, through each of its changed layouts and
refinements, always seems to have been aligned to the sunrises
at the equinoxes and the summer and winter solstices. From the
most ancient arrangements of poles of wood to the interlinked
flattened circle of trilithons, the elaborate constructions of antiquity
have always bound the patterns of sky and earth together.

All round the world the ancient peoples watched the changing specks of light in the night sky, seeing, without any magnifying equipment, patterns, animals, gods and goddesses, heroes and mythological creatures. From the farthest East to the farthest West, there is an understanding about what the stars are trying to tell us. On the most basic level the constellations of the Zodiac, for example, are simply mnemonics by which the passing seasons can be noted, so that when the ancient Egyptians saw the bright green star Sirius rising over the horizon in what is now called July, they knew that the waters of the Nile would begin to rise in the annual flood, which brought the black and fertile soil down from the mountains. Sirius is part of the constellation of the Great Dog close on the heels of Orion, the mighty hunter with his starry belt and shining sword which, after the Great Bear or Plough, is one of the easiest constellations to recognise in the winter sky.

What those scattered patterns of points of light traversing the dark heavens may have meant to our ancestors, we cannot now be sure. All round the world similar legends exist, where great human heroes or heroines have been taken up and become stars because of their exploits on earth, or where the Great Gods live out their own lives in the starry deeps of the firmament. We know that there is an ancient tradition of wisdom coming from the stars, that they have things to teach us and powers to impart. Somehow this concept has been corrupted by the mechanically minded seekers of the last few decades, and the idea of aliens from space arriving in flying saucers has taken over from a simpler and purer idea from long ago. Underneath this myth there is the seed of a great Mystery, concerning the awakening of consciousness on this planet. It is not possible to explain in words what this concept implies, but if you meditate upon the known symbolism of the stars you may uncover your own revelation. The Tarot Star card, for example, usually means 'Hope'. The stars may be used for guidance, not only in marine navigation; they may be 'wished upon', they personify the goal on which many aspiring actors and actresses set their hearts. Having 'stars in your eyes' may be a sign of love, or of ecstasy or joy. These common sayings may seem to bring us a long way from the entry of divine and starry wisdom into the Earth plane, but they retain the inner implications of a very great matter.

Even in our humblest little rites we use light, for it is most

common to light a candle before an indoor meditation, or
perhaps a nightlight in a jar for safety's sake, out of doors. A
tiny point of living flame forms a sphere of illumination and it is
the unconsidered symbolism of this which helps direct, protect
and enhance our magics. The great lights in the sky often
appear to modern people as useful rather than magical; the sun
brings daylight and the moon, if we notice her at all, changes
shape and position through the month. We can become aware
that each of these heavenly bodies gives out forces which, on the
one hand, are easily detected and on the other show more
mysterious energies, which magicians and witches through the
long ages have made use of in their workings. We know the sun
gives out heat; we bask, conditions permitting, in the warmth,
and seek out sunlight as part of most holidays. We know about
the light of the sun for it illumines our world, and through its
action everything takes on bright colours. We know about the
power of the sun being used in solar heating, yet we may forget
that every living thing draws on the sun for life. Green plants
exist and grow because sunlight assists their internal chemistry
to transmute water and minerals into greenery, flowers and
fruit.

The moon, reflecting the light of the sun from her pale
surface, draws up the tides by her monthly gravitational pull.
She rises far more erratically, sometimes seeming at the sky's
zenith, sometimes low on the horizon. We don't usually notice
such strange behaviour, finding it sufficient to cope with the
phases of waxing, full and waning, which even modern witches
take into consideration in their Goddess-based rites. Because
the human body contains about 65% water we too are drawn
by the lunar tides, but in a different way. Often, towards the
full or the dark of the moon (as people differ), our dreams
become more vivid or contain stronger images, more lasting
impressions than at other times. Those who keep dream diaries
will soon discover such a pattern emerging, and this nocturnal
awareness can be enhanced to make use of our innate predictive
abilities so that we can teach ourselves, over many months, to
dream true and gain glimpses of the future.

The moon's powers have nearly always been associated with
psychic matters, and though old pagan meetings usually took
place at the full moon, this was a purely practical matter. In the
days before street lighting or the use of calendars, most people
calculated time by the phases of the moon, and if gatherings

were to be held, the light from the moon would not only fix the date but guide the travellers to their secret destination, assuming that the sky was clear or that it wasn't raining! The real magical work was, and still is, normally done in the days leading up to both the full and new moons. If you want to increase your personal psychic powers, try experiments in the days before the new moon, when she is dark, for then her magical forces work on our inner levels. See how much more structured and controlled your meditations are then, how much easier it is to concentrate on occult work. This applies to divination with the Tarot, and the psychic aspects of healing.

Just before the full moon, work outgoing magic, so that her astral light can shine upon your healing spell, your vegetable patch or herb garden. Try to get out of doors at night and sense the power in the air and the earth under your feet. Talk to your tree and see how the moon blesses the growing things with a muted light yet an inner tidal power of growth. Learn to plant flowering plants, herbs and vegetables which are picked above the ground when the moon is waxing, and root vegetables, tubers and bulbs when she is waning, as the Wise Ones of old used to do.

You can try blessing things with moon power, by taking a glass goblet or bowl of spring water and a shiny glass mirror out during a clear night of a waxing moon. When the moon is fairly low on the horizon, newly risen or just setting, catch her light in the water, so that you can see her reflection in it. This moon-blessed water can be used to scry in, placed in a clear vessel on a dark background, perhaps contained within the circle of candle light just as the old witches used to scry in their seething cauldrons. Focus your inner sight on the depths of the water when it has become still, and then relax with your eyes closed. Ask the moon to bless your vision, and gently open your eyes, gazing steadily but without strain into the water. See what you notice, but do it in a calm way, allowing any changes to occur without breaking your detached mode of thought. Nothing may happen the first time you try, but if you persist you will begin to see a milkiness in the water, vague patterns of colour, points of light, and over a few sessions, these will grow clearer and eventually become pictures, symbols, numbers, words, figures, or simply voices in your head, telling you things. Keep the water in a dark glass bottle, keep it clean and you may drink a sip as a token of kinship with the powers of the moon, or sprinkle it over your head. It can be used to bless the room, lunar talismans and so on.

Because both the sun and the moon dictate the cycles of our lives, giving us days and nights, months, times of inwardness and bright periods of outer growth, so these forces can be invoked to help with rituals. Again, this is an exercise which needs to be practised slowly, step by step, becoming familiar with every part, and then you will discover that you can perform the whole thing, mentally, quickly and effectively.

Sit quietly in your favourite place, best of all out of doors under a great tree, and on the first occasion bring a notebook. In this you will need to write a list of concepts and instructions, and as you go through the ritual, if you are doing it right, you will be given a set of short poems, invocations, sayings, call them what you will, to make your very own personal space-blessing ceremony. This simple exercise is known as 'Calling the Light' and is a very ancient way of building a magical sphere about you, to enhance your magic, bring you peace of mind or as a protection from the scurrying vibes of the everyday world. It should only be seen as a temporary measure, to cope with a brief problem, not a suit of incorruptible armour to be worn all the time.

Begin by looking to the East. Think of the sun at sunrise. See the sky is already light, but over the dark rim of the horizon a point, then a bar of brilliant light is appearing, until the great circle of the golden sun can be seen rolling upwards into the sky. See this clearly and acknowledge the dawn with a small poem or saying. Next look to the South and see banks of bright red, orange and yellow flowers vibrant with sunlight, warmth and energy. Visualise it until you can feel the heat, smell the flowers, hear the bees busy in the blossoms. Write another poem or invocation to the sun at noon. Perceive everything flooded with light. Next look to the West, and the setting sun in the apricot and azure sky of evening. Feel the power sinking into the Earth or the Western ocean. Sense the coolness descending, and awaken peace and contentment and satisfaction within your heart. Write words of farewell to the light, and welcome to the enfolding darkness. To complete this circle, look to the North and see a rocky landscape at night under a sky studded with millions of bright and multicoloured stars. Call upon the powers of those stars to inspire and awaken your inner wisdom. Feel the entire energy of the universe slowly turning about you, and write star-spangled words of longing for your galactic home, your Cosmic Mother and Sky Father. See the blackness and brightness, live in that sky.

Next, look to your right, and in the imagined darkness of night, see the pale crescent of the new moon rising. Call her sister, lover or friend and ask that her light will shine on your dreams and awaken your mystical powers. See her rise up among the singing stars, and write words to speak of that experience. Next look to your left and there see the old moon setting, again a pale crescent, mirror image of the new moon. See faintly against the dark night sky the starlit filament of curving light which traces the new moon in the old moon's arms, as they sink silently into the West. Ask for inner strength when things are difficult, patience, endurance and persistence so that no matter how dark events may look, you will always know that a light will shine upon you, and a new and brighter day will dawn. Next look up, and there at the zenith of heaven is the round face of the full moon, high and poised above you. She can offer you words of illumination, of wine-bright inspiration and cold logic, even when this is least expected. Her words may sound hard in your ears for what is seen by moonlight is never the same as things seen in the light of the sun.

Next, look down. Here there seems to be no light, just utter blackness of the deep and fertile Earth. Yet here is foundation, security, the springboard from which your wildest dreams can be launched, the home to which you will eventually return at the end of all your wanderings, through this world and many others. See darkness as solid, firm and strong, feel its support. Then when light has seeped away entirely, perceive with inner sight a minute point of light, a tiny star concealed like a diamond hidden in an ebon velvet mantle. Discover the relief of that inner spark, and see all other lights of Earth being lit from such a tiny flame until they blaze and twinkle all round. Write words of blessing and thanksgiving for the all-embracing Earth.

Lastly, look within your own heart. See there too is a flame of light, the divine, eternal spark which has been part of your own essence since you came into being, and learn how that is part of the Creator, and through this all your magical power can be extended. If you become aware that you are connected to the source of energy which powers the entire universe you will see that you can do anything your true will requires. It is by this

slender link that whatever powers of magic you learn to control
flow into the realm of Earth and take effect, making cures,
moving mountains or aiding humanity on its long road of
evolution. If that link is clear and well-established you will
never be tired by your magic, for you cannot exhaust the power
of the universe! You should always draw from that divine spark
within, to refresh yourself and be full of joy and peace at the end
of any working. Write a final line praising this hidden light
within that it may come to shine as a beacon of love and truth
and honour among living beings of Earth.

You will see, if you draw a diagram of what has been
described above, that you have created a circle about you,
marking the horizon, and then a circle from your right hand,
over your head and down under the ground, and within this is
that divine spark at your heart centre. This is a most ancient
and potent symbol, a sphere delineated in white flame, the
Inner Light, the Fire of Creation, the Illuminator, the
Enlightening Wisdom. The ancient Egyptians had a whole set
of prayers following the cycle of Ra, their Sun God, right
through his circular progress from sunrise through the heavens
to sunset, and finally through the lower regions of darkness, and
all the while he was perceived to change from flying solar hawk
to dark scarab-headed Lord of the Otherworld. Meditate well
on each part of this progress, and you will be inspired to create
your own prayers or invocations for 'Calling the Light', and it
will bring a great deal of power to all the work you do.

Outwardly you should be trying to work with the monthly
lunar cycles and finding ways of celebrating the actual
interactions of the Sun and the Earth, the first flowers, the
harvests, the time of clearing out, the tide of growth and
expansion in the world. Our seasons may be changing because
of the perilous effects humanity's activities have had on the
ozone layer, the gases in the upper atmosphere, and pollution of
earth, water and the air about us, but we must learn to keep
step with Mother Nature, changing with her if necessary. We
must watch carefully for the first signs of spring, be they early
or late, for the harvests in the fields or the gardens and
orchards, and in our urban way, probably, celebrate the life
force of Nature. And by our prayers, our rituals and
celebrations, perhaps we can begin the heavy task or reversing
some of the harm that has been done to our planet, from which
we are born and to which we are kindred. Become aware of how

you live, what you use, what you buy and what you throw away. Every single effort at recycling, tree planting, care of the environment, the wildlife, the birds, butterflies and beetles could be the single event which reverses the worldwide trend, rebalances the planet to healing and growth. Think hard and act gently.

Throughout each week begin to align yourself to the power of the planets, those wandering stars long ago noticed by our mystical ancestors. Every Sunday give a thought to the nuclear fusions which power the sun in the sky, and the green environment below. See how the sun is a force for healing of the body, of the earth and of enlightenment of the spirit. Light one gold or yellow candle and work for a specific healing of a friend or loved one, if they have asked for help, or for the world and all its sick children. Ask that the light of knowledge may fall upon those who can change things at national and international levels, that harvests may be adequate, that they may be fairly distributed, that sufficient rain falls to restore the rivers.

On Monday, light two silver or white candles and work on the psychic aspect of yourself, or on the feminine aspect of any male practitioner. Try to accept intuition and hunches, those subtle hints of action or inaction, which can make so much magic work. It is the moon-led certainty which encourages your abilities to divine, to read the Tarot, to find hidden water or the seat of illness. Learn to trust the inner senses and welcome their intervention in any situation. Use Mondays as a time to enhance your dreams and align yourself with inner visions.

Tuesday is governed by the red planet, Mars, god of war and conflict, yet also ruler of energy, enthusiasm and strength. His number is five, and his sword can be protective as well as aggressive. Learn to draw on his courage, his power to seek the right in any quarrel. Be willing to find that you are wrong, that you have misused information or misjudged a situation, and then become Mars-brave and apologise, often much harder than defending a wrong point of view.

Wednesday is flighty Mercury's day for all forms of travel and communication. He may be invoked with eight orange candles, to help you write well, compose music or love letters, speak clearly before a vast audience or to impress a potential new boss at a job interview. He can help you reconnect with lost friends or strangers on your wavelength and, by most mysterious ways, find out-of-print books or rare videos, and the phone numbers of long-lost uncles! He is also the pagan saint of thieves so watch out, his services might cost you something which goes missing or, in a playful mood, he could restore to you something you mislaid ages ago.

Thursday heralds the power of materialistic Jupiter, father of the gods, in his royal-blue limo with cedarwood trimmings! He is the jolly ruler of wealth and growth of financial situations. His number is four and his power is the foursquare function of monetary stability and success at hard work. He cannot be bribed and will not gamble but he will repay all debts in due course, and can be requested to help with increasing your material position so long as you are willing to work for what you require. He helps with plans and designs and, being a very large planet, does not move swiftly but keeps his word in the end.

Green Lady Venus rules Fridays, partnerships and love affairs and looks after children and the growing things of Nature, rather than money. She brings about long-term healing, especially where there is a growth in understanding brought about by coming to terms with the illness or problem affecting our lives. Her number is seven, and she shows her power in often uncontrolled passions, of love, joy, ecstasy and even as the green-faced goddess of envy. She will not call an unwilling partner to your bed, nor change anyone's mind against her will, but she can teach everyone to become worthy of love, and gently guide each to find an ideal partner, for work, companionship or sexual enjoyment. She too demands that we work at our relationships and will not let us find quick solutions to affinities or love affairs until we have earned such a reward by working in her gardens, making beautiful her realm.

Saturdays come under the dark thrall of black Saturn, old man of the gods, keeper of boundaries, lord of time, ruler of old age and death and the Otherworld, for he also keeps the keys to the portals between this world and the other. Unless we come with patience and speak with respect, he will not listen to our hasty pleas for help or guidance. Like an ancient grandfather of all living he is steeped in ageless wisdom but can be crotchety and, like the dark Moon Goddess who is his magical counterpart, he can be sharp with his answers. His number is three, his metal lead, his incense myrrh. He is the generous giver of stability, the comforter of the aged, for he shows their inherited wisdom, distilled through a long life, in its bright glory.

Every planet teaches us valuable lessons, as it taught those who watched these coloured planets move through the sky aeons ago. We have to relearn their varied wisdoms, reopen the doors they hold closed, ask as children of the universe the eternal questions, the need for help or information or specific powers to deal with individual needs. Each can be summoned with the right colours, numbers (there are variations between systems, but all work!), metals or shapes and incenses, which you will learn by book research, direct inspiration or pure guesswork. Build up tables of correspondences so that you can make small charms with appropriate tree leaves or flowers, or complex talismans, inscribed traditionally on virgin parchment with the quill of the relevant bird, if you so wish (although new felt-tip pens of the right colour are a lot easier, especially when applied to tinted paper with a smooth finish!). Learn to combine the energies of two planets for each spell, write simple chants or elegant poetry to make your request clear, precise and reasonable. For healing, perhaps the Sun and Venus, gold writing on green paper cut into a circle (a one-sided figure for the sun), made on a Friday and blessed and put to work on Sunday by the light of one gold (or seven green) candles. Burn frankincense for the Sun and rosepetals for Venus, so that your plea is carried aloft to the other planes where the seeds of healing may be planted. Then forget about it, so that like a seed sown in the garden it may safely develop in secret and darkness, until it is ready to reach out into the light of our day.

Exercises

By now you should have seen many of the changing phases of the sun and moon, spending mornings and evenings watching the sky, feeling their powers. You will have seen the seasons change and perhaps, in simple ways, celebrated the old feasts.

In your Book of Illumination make a list of thirteen moons, giving each one a name, like Snowdrop Moon or Oak Tree Moon, of your own choosing. Describe tasks to fit into each one, some which you have accomplished already, others which you hope to do later this year or next, when you repeat the cycle on a higher arc.

Read something about basic astrology, and draw up a diagram of the twelve signs of the Zodiac, their ruling planets, the colours, numbers and ideas you associate with them. Add incenses, flowers growing in their month, trees, animals, symbols, elements, and as many attributes as you can find. Meditate on each sign for three sessions, if you can, asking the actual stars to teach you their significance, and add that knowledge to your chart.

Make a lantern which will hold a small candle, set in plaster perhaps, or a nightlight inside a jar so that it won't blow out at outdoor meditations or rites. Find four candlesticks or make these for the four quarters. You can even try making some candles too.

Compare your dreams from the waxing half of the moon to those in the waning half. Compare the results of your meditations, looking back at the early entries in your Book.

How can you use the power of the moon through a whole month to heal one person? How would you use her light to improve your divinations?

Try making moon-blessed water, and write a short poem or prayer to the moon in all three phases to ask for her help. What is the fourth phase? What would it be good for, in magical workings?

Try moon scrying in a home-made black mirror.

Find a moon bowl of clear glass which you can paint black outside, for scrying or using moon water to bless things.

Write a short ritual to use on the night of the new moon, and one for the full moon, asking for help with the kinds of magic you would work in each fortnight. Begin it with 'Calling the Light' and practise that until you can do it from memory. Use it six times in this moon for inner journeys, imagining that you are following the sun over the horizon into the Underworld, and then the moon up into the night sky. Record the results of these very powerful journeys.

Imagine yourself going back through time to a full moon gathering of old-fashioned country folk. Seek out their 'Man in Black' or 'Maiden of the Revels' and see what happens.

Draw up a chart of the seven planets, their days and all the symbols, colours, numbers, incenses and other information you can find. Try out some simple two-planet talismans, using coloured paper and new pens. There are lots of ways you can experiment with the material here, because you will surely be guided as to what you need to know.

Here are just a few books:

Dion Fortune, *The Sea Priestess* and *Moon Magic* (both novels) (Aquarian)

Dolores Ashcroft Nowicki, *First Steps in Ritual* (Aquarian)

Michael Howard, *Earth Magic* (Hale)

Doreen Valiente, *The Rebirth of Witchcraft* (Hale)

Janet and Stewart Farrar, *Life and Times of a Modern Witch* (Hale)

Marian Green, *The Elements of Ritual Magic* (Element Books)

11.

RECOVERING THE ANCIENT WISDOM

Having reached the state where you are able to imagine yourself without body, thoughts or imagination, to activate those databanks you should then strive to sense the process by which you gain experience. Imagine yourself building up a personality and sending it forth into incarnation. As you do so, you will find certain images associated with the incarnation begin to arise . . . they are pointers to far memories which are worth checking. . .

J H Brennan: *The Reincarnation Workbook*

In times past, those who followed the work of the village witch or Cunning Man started gaining their knowledge from their cradles, learning by watching, questioning and taking part in all those tasks wherein the psychic skills are developed and brought into controlled use. Today we gain our knowledge away from home, at school, from books, TV programmes, and videos and, I suppose these days, from computers. Little of this knowledge involves the dimension of *experience*, so vital to the practical arts of magic. You can learn *how* from a book, where, even when, but you cannot turn that information into real understanding without *doing* it. Most practical knowledge is remembered because of what we did, rather than what we saw or heard. Children left to play naturally will mimic the actions of their elders. They may not understand the principles of architecture, but given bricks or sand they will build houses or castles. Others will make mud pies, or imaginary food out of leaves and water. They may act out the cooking process without the adult knowledge about the production of heat by gas or electricity. That is exactly how the children of the Wise Ones gained their knowledge. Acting out herb brewing, scrying in a pool or puddle, talking to trees and birds and animals, and *realising they got answers* was how they gained experience. We don't even talk to each other half the time, let alone question a tree about the weather prospects – we watch the TV weather forecast!

We have lost the simple, playful interaction with Nature or with several generations of our ancestors. We may scarcely have known our grandparents, perhaps because of family rifts or because by the time we were mature enough to value the words of the aged, they were far away or in a home, or dead. It may have been cramped when families with six or more children, parents and several grandparents crammed into one house but without the distraction of modern entertainment systems, they had to talk, sing and share tales as a form of relaxation. The oral and folk song tradition survived in many places until the First World War. Then, not only were many young men killed but the dances and songs, the traditions they would have found in the country, were killed also. For example, much of the Morris dancing tradition only survived because the stay-at-home sisters, wives and mothers of the young men dancers had watched the steps and learned the music, so it fell to them to remember and teach the post-war generation. Many of the best dancers, quite old men now, were taught this mens' Mystery by the womenfolk.

Much of our vast folk tradition had already been wiped out, not only by religious fervour but by political change. Under the austere years of the Commonwealth singing and dancing and the celebration of festivals was stamped upon. Many of the ancient, beautiful glass windows, the pagan images, the statues of saints, the wall decorations and holy trees were destroyed, and the gatherings about maypoles and wells were prohibited. For about sixty years all these folk customs were repressed, just long enough for many of them to be forgotten or not revived. Luckily, many have been over the years; others are being recalled and brought back into annual calendars of many villages and towns. They may start off as ways of attracting visitors to the area, but those involved often recapture the essence of the event, and its magical spirit turns a village fête into a really powerful and unifying event.

Folklorists, researchers, historians and genealogists are delving deeper every day into the written, painted, sculpted and embroidered records of our history. They are tracing the meanings of village names, the roots of calendar customs, the meaning of superstitions and the lines of families back for many hundreds of years. All this information could well be of use to the trainee witch or student shaman; the hours spent in the local reference library can make up for the years of childhood tied up with sports teams or school work, or watching TV, whereas our ancestors would have been following their parents and grandparents through their daily grind, learning on the job. Look through parish records, for there you may find details of your own forebears, their homes and trades, and who knows, some of them may have been herbalists, gardeners, horse-copers, farmers or specialists at any of the trades which had their inherent magic and secrets. If you don't look you will never know for sure what mystic blood may be flowing in your veins!

Another line of enquiry is pursued much more secretly by magicians, occultists and people interested in self-analysis. This is the research into past lives, or far memory as it was called by Joan Grant, whose 'reincarnationary novels' tell of her previous lives in ancient Egypt, Greece and among the Red Indians in North America. She was one of the first people seriously to study her own past and her books *Winged Pharoah* and *Scarlet Feather* have given many ordinary people an insight into the idea that each of us has an immortal spirit which not only returns to earth in a different body, but has actually retained the memory of that continuous existence. It only requires the correct technique, time, patience and a reliable companion to uncover some of that stored information.

As with many aspects of the ancient wisdom, there are 'instant techniques', crash courses in 'past life recall', 'regression' or 'time travel', some of which work reliably, and some which can lead to ego trips, personality disorders and confusion on the part of the seeker and power play on the part of the facilitator. It is not a matter for amateurs to play with, nor is it something you should attempt until you have been working on the basic magical techniques of meditation and so on for at least a year. You need to know a lot about your own inner life before you begin probing about and stirring up the mud at the bottom of the lake of far memory. It is also well worth spending any spare time in your probationary studies learning something of the social history, the workings of the state and state religion, the changes of kings and rulership, of your own land and of any others which interest you. If you do start delving into the past at some later time, or trying one of the safe and basic methods described later on here, it will help to know when each king or queen was on the throne, or what the religions of the world worshipped, and when they were founded.

Today there is a great upsurge in interest in shamanism, seeing it as a variation on the theme of village witch or community wise man, but the roots of the tradition are very different. To become a shaman, or shamanka to use the proper feminine form, you have to nearly die. That is one factor which most of those professing to be shamans overlook. You do not become a shaman by initiation or by teaching, or by someone else telling you that you are, or could be, one. You have to have suffered a near-death experience, life-threatening illness or accident during which the inner powers led your dissected body up the Tree of Life and showed you how you would only be healed if you become a shaman and serve your tribe. You would serve the tribe as a healer only by bringing power through from the land of the dead, by entering a deep, near-death trance, seeking the soul of the sick person, and fighting the spirits in the Otherworld to bring it back to life. It wasn't a matter of dancing around a bit, chanting a few rhymes or waving wands, crystals or feathers over someone. Those are all modern ideas attached, probably wrongly, to magical arts from older civilisations. The historical shamans came from Siberia and were individuals who only took up their calling after fighting off a serious illness, and what they could do for their own simple community was a result of discovering how to save their own lives, by talking to the spirits of the dead.

Similarly, witches in Britain and Europe didn't belong to covens, have High Priests and Priestesses leading them complex rituals eight times a year and at full moons. There is no evidence from the history of villages that covens or groups of witches existed. Only in the witch persecutions in Scotland, where witnesses were tortured, was there any suggestion that witches met or worked magic in groups. There is no evidence at all of regular celebrations, although there are many pre-Christian customs set at the beginning of May and the end of October which echo parts of what modern witches do. The contemporary arts of coven witches and the set rituals they attend were written largely by Doreen Valiente and Gerald Gardner in the 1950s. Some newer versions, using festivals called Litha and Mabon, were invented by Alex Sanders and his followers in the 1960s.

Doreen Valiente has written many excellent books on aspects of the Crafts which she learned from many sources, including the village witches of her native Sussex, described in her first book *Where Witchcraft Lives*, now, I believe, out of print. She points out that there are many simple spells, arts and bits of folk magic too trivial to be written out by the medieval scholars who formalised much of cermonial magic, with its Hebrew and Latin roots. Old spells included making 'witch bottles' full of pins or coloured threads, keeping harm at bay; stopping gossip by creeping up behind the tell-tale and sticking an iron nail through her shadow, or leaving open scissors or crossed knives on your doorstep so that no evil could enter. One charm used a snail pinned to a thorn tree to cure warts.

The oldest charms often used thorns to 'prick the conscience of those who wished you harm' by naming a leaf and sticking prickles through it, or by binding a red cord around a bundle of rushes, named after someone who was maligning you. The Witch Museum in Boscastle, Cornwall, used to be full of traditional amulets made of stone or clay, wax images used to heal or curse, and haunted stick figures still imbued with the power given them hundreds of years ago. Spells wrapped in magical red flannel containing simple verses written on parchment, with bits of hair or nail clippings to link them with the person for whom help is sought, are often turned up in boxes up the chimneys of old cottages. Mummified cats or the skeletons of hares are unearthed beneath the hearth stone, or the door step, traces of protective rites going back before the Romans, or holy, holed flints hung with red ribbons over the stable doors, alongside the horseshoe, points up, to prevent the animals being lamed or over-ridden. These were, and still are, the arts of the lone country witch who practises his or her arts secretly, at night, in the bat-flittering, owl-sounded safe places of the wilderness where Pan still plays his pipes and the Moon Maiden enchants us with her song.

These are the traces you may find in local museums, if you poke about the dusty showcases. These are the old ideas which some of the learned journals of folklore have commented upon in their crusty articles for the last hundred years or so. These are the clues to the web of traditional green folk magic, which has threads in every village, and old sacred centres as the hubs. Spells about the weather may be found in books on local peculiarities; or how winds may be tied as knots in a cord and

were sold to sailors to speed their journeys; how rain might be
called down, or kept away; and the old method of whistling for a
wind, recalled in the rhyme 'A whistling woman or a crowing
hen, Ain't no use to gods nor men!' Raising storms to sink ships
may have been part of the old arts but today's witches try spells
to prevent roads going through ancient sites, or rail tunnels
disrupting rare woodlands. Underneath, there is a common
thread of caring for the community. Not all spells were or are
carefully thought out; some will do more harm than good, some
will bring unfortunate results or short-term gains leading to
longer term losses. If you try out magical spells you will soon
learn what can and can't be done, what charms and chants
work, and which bring only the sure answer that that working
will fail and an understanding of why that will be so.

Most witches, or rather those who were accused and
convicted of witchcraft, were hanged, so if you delve into past
lives and find yourself on a bonfire, either you are misleading
yourself or you are undergoing the penalty in Scotland or
Europe, or were accused of heresy. Witch-finders were paid to
bring people to trial, but most of those who met their fate on the
gallows were social outcasts of their day. The real Wise Women
and Cunning Men should have been well aware of any such
mortal danger, and found ways of going into hiding. Those who
were accused were tried in courts speaking Latin, the official
language of the courts and the Church, and would have
understood little of what was going on. In England they were
not allowed to be tortured, only kept awake for nights on end,
made to stand or squat in one position. Any small animals or
flies were thought to be familiars. Those who were convicted, on
evidence usually from insulted neighbours or those with a local
grudge, were hanged and often buried at a crossroad (which was
actually sacred in pagan terms, being the place of the dark
Goddess, Hecate) outside the Church's hallowed grounds.

Do some historical research into what really did go on, and
you will find that medieval England was very different from the
ideas put forth by some 'past life recallers', who can tell you
about being burned at the sake as a witch, having joined in
coven meetings at Stonehenge and the like! Also remember,
most of the records of the witch trials were issued by those who
were convinced that individuals were really evil-doers, in league
with the Devil, capable of causing sickness, blasting crops or
raising storms. They were determined to find a victim and

bring him or her to the gallows, and those accused had no counsel for the defence and probably little idea of what was going on. The Inquisition, setting out to find 'heretics' come what may, even had a list of improbable accusations against which those brought to the test were questioned. Most of the questions were impossible to give a right answer to; for example, victims were asked 'Do you believe in the Devil?' If they said 'Yes' because that was what the Church, who invented the Devil, wanted them to say, they were accused of Devil worship, If they said 'No', the real pagan answer, they were convicted of heresy, for doubting the teaching of the Church. It was a no-win situation. However, it is extremely unlikely that many real 'witches' were caught, especially if you examine the answers some gave.

There is no hint of pagan beliefs, no concensus of opinion about covens, there is no mention of female priestesses leading rituals, no word about spells or magic, even. In Scotland some were made to speak of a 'man in black', supposed by writers like Margaret Murray to be some sort of high priest or master of a coven, but there isn't a lot to go on. Certainly there are a few surviving old family groups in Britain where the Magister, a male leader, is the one who arranges seasonal festivals and magical gatherings, but even these few such modern 'men in black' might find it hard to prove their ancient heritage didn't come from a book on the witch trials, or was a fairly recent idea, dreamed up to give them greater power than the usual leader, the female High Priestess, whose word is law.

Whatever historians have recovered by their literary researches and discovered from tales or folk superstitions about the old ways, there is a great deal of valuable material to be recovered by those who wish to reawaken their heritage. As has been said before, no learning or knowledge can ever be completely lost. It may well be deeply buried, it may be fragmentary, it may be found in many local traditions, with widely scattered fractions being part of the seasonal or calendar feasts in certain places, making it hard to see the whole rite or celebration in its entirety, but somewhere all old wisdom can be retrieved. If you begin with a bit of ordinary historical research, taking all that you read with a pinch of salt but meditating on any common themes, or the kinds of gut reaction you may instinctively have about certain ideas, then you may be able to gradually rediscover the old ways.

One very simple method which is quite safe because it does not suggest that *you* are reliving a past life, but are merely observing what may have happened at a certain time or place, is to take a festival and initially 'invent' a scenario. For example, in the winter, try one of the Yuletide feasts. Imagine an old hall house decked with greenery, smell the baking bread, the joints of meat roasting over an open fire, the stewing cauldron of broth. Hear the voices of the common folk, gathering for the feast, see their costumes, the colours and textures of their clothes, hear any songs or tales being told around the fire, as all await the evening meal. Imagine yourself as one of the lowly villagers sharing this annual celebration. See what you can experience of all that goes on. Imagine the Wise Ones of the community going out into the cold darkness to perform their own special rituals to call back the power and heat of the sun, to welcome the Star Child, Mabon son of Modron, the Great Mother. Try to see yourself as the apprentice to such a one, a child of the magical family, learning at your grandparents' knees the arts and skills or healing spells used by them.

Build up, bit by bit over about seven evening meditations, the whole feel and atmosphere of the event. Imagine yourself being part of it, and then sit back and observe closely what goes on. Write down everything you learn, for you may need to research and check what you find out. It is no good inventing a totally wrong set of ideas and then trying to make them work, for that is a waste of effort. Be content with small or trivial details, and gradually you will discover that your inner vision and 'imagination' grows stronger, the images clearer and what you learn will make more sense.

Every month when the moon is waning, spend one evening in meditation on what the country folk used to do during that moon. See your imaginary village or manor house and the people around it, performing their usual tasks, as well as trying to discover the magical arts from the Wise Ones. Think about the crops and the livestock, the farm activities, both regular ones like milking and butter and cheese-making, grinding corn and baking bread, and those which were more seasonal, the hedging and ditching, harvesting, threshing grain, shearing sheep, ploughing and sowing, haymaking and fruit harvesting. Ask, in your invocations, that you see clearly what used to happen, and that in these gentle meditations you actually perceive what went on. Use your inner sight, learn to trust it, but still check what you see or the answers you are given.

Only by regularly sinking down into the detached view achieved in meditation will you gain the kind of control over your psychic vision which you would have been taught by the magicians of old. Learning these arts alone or with other novice friends is very difficult, especially so because you will have nothing to check your progress against, no one to say to you, 'Yes, that was a good meditation,' or 'No, you haven't got it right yet, try again.' You will have to be both pupil and teacher, yet those who lived in the old ways can show you their secret arts, if you ask nicely. Gradually your dreams will begin to unfold aspects of the past, perhaps even your own previous lives, when you are ready to judge what you see, and cast out those ego-tripping ideas or the kinds of experiences which can divide your personality or disturb your sleep. You will *know* what is right.

If you find creating pictures and the setting for the previous exercise difficult, or feel that you will be making up what you see, then you can try another approach. This is used by ceremonial magicians as part of their training, but as it is another way an individual can access lost information, it is worth learning. This way you can use any form of divination, the Tarot trumps, the hexagrams of the I Ching, even the magical trees, as doorways to new knowledge. Like all mental arts it requires that calm, relaxed and detached mode of thinking used for meditation, but this time you set out a symbol before you. It can be used in or out of doors, by day or night, and again, all you need is your initial symbol and a notebook in which to record immediately what you learn, or you can speak into a small tape-recorder if you prefer, though notes are far easier to refer back to!

If you are used to the Tarot, as most people interested in magic are these days, you will know that the pack is divided into two parts: the Major Arcana of picture cards, and the Minor Arcana, which in many of the older decks has no pictures. Many of the more recently designed packs have pictures on all cards, but to begin your exploration through the Halls of Wisdom it is the twenty-two numbered cards that should form your training method. You can either deliberately select one card or, having sorted out the Major Arcana from the deck, randomly pick a card for each experiment. What you are going to do is use that symbol as a doorway to a particular kind of ancient knowledge, so that each card represents a kind of entry ticket to a certain sort of information.

Get into your relaxed frame of mind, allow your thoughts to become still and calm and then, placing the card you have chosen where you can see it, gaze quietly upon it for a few moments. For this explanation, I have drawn a card which happens to be the Chariot. This is an excellent card for time travel as anyone, even those who know little about the significance of Tarot symbolism, will see immediately that it shows an ancient form of transport. Therefore the gate through which this particular example will take us will be concerned with that sort of magic.

Imagine now, with your eyes closed, the card depicted as large as a door, but actually painted on a curtain of stiff, white cloth. This is covering an opening in a stone wall. See the tapestry before you, larger than life, with the black and white horses and the charioteer with his Egyptian headdress and

rainbow girdle coming towards you. Smell the heat and sweat of
the animals, with the sphinx heads on their harness; hear their
hooves pounding the ground, sense it tremble beneath you,
then leap up onto that magical form of transport and be carried
in a sharp circle, back through the gate with its white curtain.
Use every part of your relaxed will to become part of that image
and experience.

You will be carried by this symbol into the age-old arts of the
folk who worked with horses and with their magic. You may
find yourself entering the forge, and see the blacksmith at work,
shaping horseshoes out of grooved metal bars, red-hot from the
fire. You may see him making a sword or ritual dagger. Ask
him questions about his ancient craft, its secrets, and because
you have arrived there in a mystical way, he will answer you.
Learn about the magics of fire, and of the quenching water,
learn about blades and the magics of division and defence.
Learn the secrets of iron, with which evil may be pinned to the
ground. Hear the stories of Wayland Smith, or even St Michael
the angel of Fire and the flame-shaped sword. Ask about the
earliest roots of those magics, when the control of fire was a
matter of life and death in the cold of the Ice Age, when
mankind had his childhood. Learn about flint and tinder, and
the making of fires, the power of candle flames, and of the sun.
All these are questions you may have answered if you happen to
select the Chariot. And there is much besides this, for there are
the magics of the horseman, to calm wild beasts, to control and
heal animals, and to speak with all creatures.

There is also the Riddle of the Sphinx, an ancient Mystery
question of 'What goes on four legs in the morning, two legs at
noon, and three legs in the evening? How many legs has it at
midnight?'. The sphinx may open a door to ancient Egyptian
magic, under the dominance of the Great Goddess, Isis, or the
protection and guidance through many worlds of the jackal-
headed Anubis.

One simple symbol can put you in touch with a vast store of
knowledge for that is what the pictures of the Tarot, or even the
more abstract hexagrams of the I Ching, portray. They are
magical talismans in their own right, keys to great books of
inner learning, if you have the time and patience to use them.
What they teach may at first be obscure, yet it is safe and can be
used many times over, until you thoroughly understand what
every one of those symbols, or the trees, can teach you. Take

your time. One regular attempt each week with a new symbol will be sufficient, for you will find that other bits of information related to what you have uncovered in this way will turn up in dreams, or spring from the pages of books. Write down all that you learn for you may be privy to knowledge which has been concealed for hundreds or even thousands of years.

Each picture of the Tarot trumps is an acknowledged source of information, that is what the system was developed for, but there is no one way of reading the cards which is true or right. Everyone must make out their own interpretation, their own understanding of what each reveals to them. Don't swallow anyone else's words until you have walked through some of these secret gates on your own, and seen them reveal their hidden wisdom to you alone. Be willing to be taught by the Source and not some biased human commentator. We are all students of those great books, and everyone of us needs to learn different lessons.

You can use images or concepts of the gods and goddesses in the same way. Conjure them up in your inner vision, perhaps starting with the sun or moon in the sky, or one of their symbols, a cauldron or white horse for the Goddess, a sword and shield or a shepherd's crook for the God.

Exercises

To gain the best results from the work in the eleventh moon you really need a reliable companion; a friend you can trust, a co-walker in the old ways, other members of the group if you are part of a coven. Not because the work is especially dangerous, though it can be scary, but because you may need someone to ask sensible questions. There are many ways of re-entering the times past and regaining information from them, but your task will be easier if, when you have carried out the deep relaxation exercise, got really switched off and then imagined that you have walked through a time tunnel, feeling the centuries unroll, someone else can ask you what you are wearing, what sort of landscape you are in, what kind of food you eat and so on. You will need to discuss the questions beforehand, and preferably have them written down. You may be asked about buildings, animals, plants and natural things, and from your studies of trees you will be able to discover the time of year, or perhaps the part of the world, if there are trees only seen on one continent. Take your time over this exercise, going a step at a time through several sessions rather than spending hours groping around in some alien timescape. Be careful; this can be a frightening experience if you arrive in the middle of a battle, or during the plague years, or in a hungry winter. What you experience will seem very real, especially if you have latched on to a previous life. Take care, step warily, and maybe you will meet up with some of the Old Wise Ones so that they can teach you or at least show you something of their forgotten knowledge.

On your own, stick to the simpler visits to the old house, and gain confidence and awareness that way. The story may continue in your dreams or during meditations on any useful information you gained. Do write notes in your Book for what you find could be valuable to others, who are similarly seeking lost knowledge.

Try the Tarot card exercise. This too could reveal extraordinary amounts of valuable information, old ideas and forgotten arts and crafts. These are all simple but actually powerful exercises so be patient, trying one thing at a time and, if necessary, leaving a few days between adventures, so that you have time to assimilate and fully understand what you see.

Call upon aspects of the Goddess to teach you, or the God, as craftsman or magician, to instruct you in his ways. They really will help, and by now you should be able to enter their wild world at will.

Here are some books which may give you further ideas:

J H Brennan, *The Reincarnation Workbook* (Aquarian)
G L Glaskin, *Windows of the Mind* (Prism Press)
C J Jung, *Man and His Symbols* (Routledge and Kegan Paul)
Helen Wambach, *Reliving Past Lives* (Arrow)
Joan Grant, *Far Memory* (Corgi)
Brian Inglis, *Trance* (Grafton)

12.

DEDICATION TO THE OLD WAYS

We must be prepared to shift the basis of all our motives if we want to receive Initiation. This requires singleness of purpose that baulks at no sacrifice – 'Sell all that thou hast and follow Me,' said the Master. . . . There is no reason why anyone should offer themselves as a candidate for Initiation, for they can achieve the goal of Divine Union by the winding path of evolution; but on the other hand, they must not declare that the ancient Secrets have been lost, because they, not being willing to pay the price, have not received the Great Pearl.

Dion Fortune: *The Training and Work of an Initiate*

One of the things which attracts quite a few people to the idea of witchcraft is that they will become 'Initiates', that they will be ritually taken into a coven, be able to work magic instantly and have all their desires met after that moment. Anyone who still holds such views will be in for a great disappointment! People see magic as a way of gaining power, and this is certainly true, but it is not 'power over', to coin a phrase used by Starhawk, but 'power from within'. 'Power over' other people, the power to change them against their will, the power to dominate, physically, mentally, astrally or even spiritually, may appear to be the goal of magic, but those are all false concepts. What the training, through all its months of steady progress, will lead you to, if you have the guts and determination, is 'power from within', and initially it can only affect you.

The first real lesson of magic which you will learn is one of disillusionment. You may start out with all kinds of ideas about witchcraft, the Old Arts, magic and occultism, but if you work at any of the exercises, even sporadically and without concentration, you will produce results. Not precisely what you aimed for, probably; you may scare yourself with what happens and your dreams may change, but as your inner sight clears you will discover that the world you have lived in all your life is actually very different from what you had always assumed. Magic is uncomfortable; its initial effects are likely to be far more fierce than those achieved by an adept, for they have had years of practice backed up by firm memories of many previous lives, spent perfecting their techniques. Magic is like golf; if you could be really good at it your Masters winner would get round in eighteen strokes, scoring a hole in one every time! No matter how good you are, there are always factors about which you know nothing, or which are beyond your control, like the weather over the golf course. Magicians and old-time witches gradually learn just how much effort any kind of activity needs. It is actually for this reason that much time has to be spent sitting around with your eyes shut, meditating, concentrating, creating visions or unravelling symbolism. These simple but unavoidable arts are the ones which lead to control over those astral forces which come into play when you plant the seeds of a spell, make a talisman, pray or perform a ritual. Only by being able to sense the effects of your actions in the Otherworld can you learn to apply more or less effort to any particular working.

The second part of making progress on the path is not receiving 'initiations' from other people, going through group degree ceremonies, collecting notches on your wand for spells performed and so on, but the genuine experience of having made contact with the Goddess and the God of the Old Religion. No one else can do this, and most ceremonies do not actually make that contact for you. You stand a far better chance of gaining true initiation, and the touch of power that that will bring with it, quite alone in a wild place when, with your knees knocking and your hand clutching the lantern shaking like an aspen, you actually encounter the High Ones face to face.

It really is important to have worked through most of these exercises and produced results before you decide to commit yourself to the path of witchcraft, whether solo or with a group. In fact, if you have been making efforts at some forms of meditation and the areas of inner analysis which such experiments require, you may well have decided that you would prefer the companionship of others, or that the lone path really does work and suits your needs. It is certainly possible to use the simple kinds of spells and talismans described earlier to make yourself known to others in the esoteric world. Like all aspects of magic, it is not enough just to do a working and then sit back and expect the Inner to turn up with your request on a silken cushion. If you seek occult friends then you will either have to go to the places where they may be found, perhaps at psychic or healing fairs or talks that the local library runs, or read announcements at the back of pagan journals (of which there are about a hundred published in the UK) covering all aspects of the Craft, magic, paganism, Earth Mysteries, healing and much more! A few of the more 'popular' varieties, dealing mainly with astrology and fortune-telling, are to be found in newsagents; the better ones, small, local or simple-format magazines and journals, need to be tracked down and are very well worth supporting.

There are even a number of occult contact magazines, but do read these first and be sure they are offering genuine pen-pals or training groups. The more simple the layout, the more likely they are to be genuine. Newspapers have always been happy to make out that witches involve children in their rituals or that they harm animals, when the opposite is the truth. To join most of the genuine training schools or covens the students have to be over 21 years of age; some won't take on people under 25. Covens do not encourage sex outside marriage or involve youngsters under the age of eighteen. They never use drugs and very seldom even smoke cigarettes, and the drinking of wine is generally part of a communion and again not used to excess. This may all seem rather dull, but real magic does not take place in this everyday world but in the inner realms and there you need your wits about you, and to have absolute control over what is happening.

There are a few evil people who operate under the guise of magic, who do involve children and do some of the things the media is all too happy to pin on every witch and shaman, but those law-breakers are a long way from the Path to the Light which lies at the heart of the Western Mysteries, on all levels. They are being hunted just as much by the real adepts and the 'esoteric police' as they are by the social services and the ordinary police force. They are also likely to come under the thrall of the Lords of Karma, and they will then have to pay for their destructive actions in full. You cannot be cruel, mistreat children or expand the drug culture without discovering that there is a threefold penalty for such disruptive behaviour. Be warned; if you dabble in selfish magic, try to curse or harm other people, take risks with drugs, alcohol or practices which common sense tells you are foolish or dangerous, then you will inevitably be caught, for karma reaches everywhere.

If you commit yourself to the Hidden Paths or walking the Old Ways you will certainly be in for some surprises. The most common of these are the feelings, which never entirely go away, of 'Why on Earth am I doing this? Why am I wearing this strange robe, talking to trees or invisible beings, thinking that "spells" can possibly work in the twentieth century?' You will often find, right in the middle of a meditation or ritual, such thoughts creeping into your head, making you feel a fool. This is a sure sign that your magic is working, for you have so certainly stepped out of your normal role in life or set aside, just for the moment, the very ordinary self to adopt that magical inner personality, that it is trying to reassert what it considers normality. It never entirely goes away, as any adepts you come across will tell you, and even after decades of participating in celebrations, speaking directly with the Old Ones, venturing into the wilderness, both without and within, this sense of amusement, of fun and wonder, never really dies. It is a recollection that you are indeed straying from the ordinary world and it should never trouble you, just provide a moment's humour when the power is coming through.

If you meet other people on the Path, look at them closely. Are they your ideal sort of folk? Do they look healthy, act as if they are happy, or are they always bragging about the power they handle, or the secrets they know? Do you believe they have really walked the road to fairyland, but somehow returned without the stars in their eyes and the spring in their step? Do you see them as kindred to the Old Ones, grandchildren of the Goddess, known and loved by her and partners in her magic? Have a good look and a good think, especially if they are inviting you to join their covens or training groups. If you have really worked at some of these exercises and made your own direct contact with the Great Ones then you would be a valuable prize to a failing occult group, adding not only new blood but new power to be drained off too. That is why I have said that any magic work which leaves you tired or worn out has not been worked properly, for you should become a clear channel for the Light to flow through, no matter how much power is required, for in the end there will still be a residue of the Light left within you. Trust your own inner feelings, which ought to be becoming more sensitive and accurate, the more you walk in the Otherworld, free and clear.

Perhaps you do seek to be an initiate above all things. Well, you can join the Companions of the Inner Way on your own, in your own sacred place, making promises you can keep, and dealing with aspects of the Goddess and the God with which you feel at home and at peace. It is not something to do today, nor tomorrow, but if you plan carefully, walking gently and preparing thoroughly, you may well find you can enter that rare companionship as a free and equal member very soon.

Every initiation consists of several distinct and equally important parts. When these ceremonies are enacted as group rituals it is inevitable that the drama of the occasion may alter or change the balance or that some parts may be shortened or omitted, and more weight given to other considerations. When you are making a personal dedication you will be able to make a timetable which allows plenty of time for everything to be done as you want it, and also sufficient free periods to await a response from the Old Ones who, after all, are the only beings who can grant true admittance to their eternal company.

You can begin to search out a suitable place and look through your diary for a day or weekend which can be largely devoted to making a permanent commitment to the magical ways. If you shy away from this great step then you are very wise; don't force yourself to take on any work that you know in your heart of hearts you are not ready for. On your own, that choice is absolutely yours. Within a group there may be pressure to make up the numbers before a particular feast, or balance the males and females in a coven. Some newcomers are just too keen for their own good, wishing to rush into initiation helter-skelter without realising the seriousness of the step, or what is actually involved.

As an alternative you may, if you feel ready, undertake a ceremony of dedication, rather than an initiation. The true initiation may spontaneously occur during the working, if you are prepared and the Goddess is willing to have you reborn as her child, within her Family of the Mysteries. A dedication is an individual and personal act wherein you promise to follow a particular path of your own choice, realising how serious this step may be, for the good of the work and for as long as that work may take. In return for your offer of time, effort and love

of the Tradition, you will gain support from the Old Ones, safe
guidance in the inner realms, training, power and the ability to
heal, for example. These are all skills which you have by
birthright yet you need help and encouragement in bringing
them into practical and controlled use. You will also gain a true
companionship, both visible and invisible. There are many
seekers on different parts of the Path, many walkers in the Old
Ways, and once you join that company their presence will be
made known to you, and yours to them. You may well discover
familiar faces will suddenly reveal a new appearance for they
too have walked the Fairy Path, the Starlit Road and, without
ever speaking of such things, have already offered you
companionship, trust and friendship, but until your admittance
you have seemed as strangers.

Thousands of people are dedicated or are initiates of the
inner way in Britain nowadays. Few of those who take their arts
seriously will be wearing badges saying 'I am a Witch' or 'Born
Again Oracle'. They live their lives, as you might have to do, in
two parts, with one face for the world and the other, inner,
hidden face always turned towards the secret starlight. They
have learned the power of silence, of the kept word and
unbroken promises. They have seen things and experienced
things which few ordinary folk would comprehend or credit as
being true. They have entered the Otherworld and returned
safe, many times. They have supped with gods, woven magical
spells and brought about changes in the fabric of the world.
They are doing it now, working by day and night, healing,
mending, bringing about peace after conflict, unseen, yet
perhaps next door to you, or in the house along the road. The
ones who demonstrate their magical connections by their dress
or badges, the mystical rings or whispered hints of secrets are
either young souls who are playing, as children do, at things
beyond their years, or they are fakes, acting out a fantasy of
what they think a witch should be like, or how magicians should
behave. Look hard at them and see if you want to be like them.
It is your choice. There are many who have taken oaths of
silence and keep them, not because of threats but because they
value what they have learned and cherish it in their hearts.
They do not wish to brag about the successes they have had, or
the failures which even the most experienced sometimes have,
because they are working as agents for the Old Ones, the
Creative Power on Earth, not for self-aggrandisement or show.

Another misconception about initiation is that it is immediate, and that at the completion of the ritual you will be an instant adept and all the forces of the universe will now bow to your whim. What has actually happened is that you have been given an entrance to a new school. You may have dressed up in the uniform, been given a new satchel full of fascinating books and sources of knowledge, but you are still outside the gates and have not passed your final examinations and gained your certificate of proficiency. Many years of hard and consistent work lie ahead, just as would be needed to pass through junior, secondary and senior college, and to become really good, you need your Masters Degree in Magic, gained within the University of the Cosmos.

Becoming dedicated is an early step. It is a genuine request for guidance, and an attempt on a personal level to connect with the great powers of the universe, and to gain communion with the gods and goddesses of the land. You will need to know about making a magical circle and the use of the Elements to bless it. You need a private and special place, and a staff to use as an altar. You need to have spent many months building up the Sphere of Light so that you can do it from memory, almost without thinking, and be aware that you are in a protected place and feel safe and confident. These are the absolute preliminaries, and if you think you know enough or can leave out these vital early stages, then you are either a fool or too foolhardy for your own good. There is no advantage in rushing, any more than it would do you any good entering a marathon race if you had only ever run for a bus in training!

Initiations or rites of dedication should begin with a vigil, preferably all night. You will have to sort this out with your family because it is the first test of your ability to keep secrets. You will need to find a place where you can sit under the stars and ask for help and power and instruction. You need to review your aims and magical ambitions, your sincerity towards service of the Old Ones, and conviction that this is the first step on a path you intend to follow, perhaps at first alone, and later on in the company of others. It is a chance to resolve all doubts, or to be willing to give in to them, so that you don't take a step which you might not be ready for, or might later regret. It is also a time to find your magical name. Although you are working on your own, you are going to be reborn into the Old Ways, and as such you will become a child again!

In the Old Tradition the magical name was never that of a god or goddess (or a collection of them, as is all too common among American witches and others) but was often almost a nick-name. (Old Nick is another title of the Horned God!) Some names are those of plants, trees, animals or perhaps semi-precious stones. It could be an anagram of your own initials, or a variation of one of your ordinary given names. The less dramatic the name that comes to you at this time, the more likely it is to be a genuine 'sending', that is, a message from the Goddess. This name should be absolutely secret, and only ever used on talismans. If you ever hear that name being called, you know it is the Great Ones who are demanding your attention. Sit silently, unprotected by magical circles and really *think*, all night, under a growing moon. This is your last chance to remain an ordinary human being!

If in the morning you are convinced that dedication is the right move, then you will need to set about your preparations for that. Have a bath and cast into the water cleansing herbs and calming ones. Bask in that and become refreshed, even if you have been awake all night. Later in the day, take a picnic to eat after your dedication, as you should fast beforehand if you are following the old way closely. (This is as near an ordeal as most modern people get during the ceremony, but something more weighty may well occur soon afterwards.)

Stage Two is the making of a promise. This is not an oath with spectacular penalties which you may have read about in books, but a sincere and heartfelt promise to try to be a better human being, to develop your unique and inborn talents for the benefit of the gods on Earth. It is a promise to study and work and help those who seek aid, or to be honest with them and say what they ask is beyond your trainee powers. It is to realise the value of wisdom and ancient knowledge which you may gradually be gaining, and the responsibility of having the powers of divination. You must speak truth, but gently, so that the listener is not alarmed. These and many more are the ideas which you should promise to uphold. You should promise to keep silent, too, on those fragments of the Old Ways which could put power into the hands of the foolish or unprepared, yet you should also be willing to share your knowledge with others who are ripe to receive it.

Go to your special place, taking a candle lantern, something to eat and drink, a pen and a piece of clean paper, a sharp needle, your magical staff and some string to make a seasonal garland, and if you have one, your magical robe or a new garment and a pair of sandals which can become your occult outfit. With a handful of twigs, brush a circle of clear space in which you can lie flat with your collection of things beside you. This is one of the few occasions when you lie down during magic! When you feel ready, mentally 'Call the Light', and then light the candle lantern, placed at the foot of your altar staff.

Lay down flat on your back beside it, close your eyes and think of sinking into the Earth. With any luck after a few minutes, this will become a very strange sensation, as if the earth is moving under you, almost rocking like the sea. Concentrate on becoming part of the Earth and dying to your old life. Cast off bad habits, failures, regrets and old grudges. Empty yourself of worries; pour out your sadness, your loneliness, your grief into the Earth below until you feel hollow. This may take some time, it may make you cry, it may feel very peculiar, but it is part of the work. Discover how leaden and relaxed you are, how cool and dead you may feel, and how cleansed of old contamination.

Having died and been laid to rest, think of the seas and rivers, and springs and pools. Wash clean your sparkling inner self, and float gently in the waters of birth. Be at peace, drift, now allowing the new name to flow into your consciousness. Feel a sprinkling of water and a quiet voice saying 'In the name of the Living Oceans and of Pure Springs I baptise you .... May you receive blessing thereby.' Allow this to sink in fully, then you will feel as if you are drifting to the shore, on a sunlit beach or bright riverbank.

Gradually curl up into a foetal position, for you are named and about to be reborn of the Waters of Life into the Fire of Light. When you are ready, sit up, with your knees bent and your arms wrapped round them and your head bowed. Relax and begin to contemplate Fire, the Sun and his power as Sky God, the Hunter and Protector, Lord of Two Worlds. Think of your Earth Mother and slowly imagine yourself being reborn, gently, into the Light, represented by the lantern. Now take up the pen and carefully write out your promise, starting 'I .... (put your ordinary name) promise . . .' (state only things you will really try to keep) and end up with the old magical motto, 'I desire To Will, To Dare, To Know and To Keep Silent, in my new name .... I so promise.'

Now kiss the paper and burn it. Also pull out a few hairs and burn them over the flame of the candle. If you burn your finger, that is all right too. You should also prick the little finger of your left hand with the clean needle and squeeze a few drops of blood onto the Earth to symbolise the blood of birth flowing between you as a permanent bond. You may feel quite shaky at this moment so be still, with your eyes closed, and continue to sense that all is going well, and that your promise has been accepted.

The last part of this working is to breathe in new life. Take some really deep breaths and if you so wish, sing or chant or hum your new name. This may go on for some time, allowing any tensions that have built up to dissipate. You need to deepen the state of your relaxation even more for you will be entering the Otherworld and meeting the Goddess or the God who will confer upon you their sacred kinship. Sink deeper and create vividly in your mind's eye the gateway between the trees, or across the waves, or into any other aspect of wilderness where you would greet your Great Ones. Remember, they were the First Parents, the Primal Ones, and you can be as a child to them again if you trust yourself enough to let go of this reality and enter theirs.

I cannot tell you what you might encounter in this time, whether it be a brief moment or hours of clock time. I can only say that if you are sincere, and are committed to walking the Old Way, then you may well gain an experience which differs from all others in this life. If you have already been through initiation ceremonies within a group you may have had some sort of revelation, but this is rare. When it does occur those seekers are satisfied and do not need to go on to other paths. Whatever does happen to you, if the Old Ones accept you and you genuinely acknowledge them as your Lady and Lord, they may teach you their secret names, in exchange for yours. They may open within you, sharply and painfully, the psychic abilities to see true, to divine in running water and in smoke, to heal, to sing the old, lost magical songs, write poetry or beautiful ritual words. They may take something from you, leaving you bewildered and in darkness. I cannot say, for each of us is different. That is our unique value to those of the Otherworld. You will certainly *know* absolutely that you have been accepted, and that will be enough.

Perhaps you will need a few moments of rest for now is the time to eat your food, bread or fruit or cake, and drink your wine or juice and spring water, always scattering a few crumbs to others of Nature's children, and pouring a libation of thanks for what you have gained. Be still, be patient and allow whatever has happened, whether it was wild and dramatic or dark and deep within you, to assimilate. It will provide much material for you to mull over in the next few weeks.

Gradually collect your wits and say 'Thank You!' You will certainly have received something to be grateful about – if you haven't, you just weren't ready or sincere. Allow the Sphere of Light to drift away, again offering thanks for the peace and protection it brought you. At the end, be aware that the tiny spark of Light which is within you is now burning brighter. Slowly get up, scattering more bread or seeds, take the garland from your altar staff and hang it on a tree or cast it into the river, depending where you are. Think of all the work you have to do, for you are taking on the power of magical responsibility, which is a great burden for you cannot act without due consideration of all the consequences. As you sow so will you reap, so learn to refine your seed ideas and demands, so that you produce a crop you can handle.

The ritual can be gently brought to a close by saying prayers for guidance for yourself and the courage to fulfil the promises you have made. You can ask for world peace, for solutions to the ecological problems, hunger, despair, pollution and healing for those parts of the Lady's mantle which have been ruined by careless and greedy people. Give out the last ripples of power to healing the Earth, and so its human burden. Get up and stretch. You are stepping into a new life and will begin to see the world differently. Your dreams may be vivid and impulsions start to flow through your mind. You will be led into all sorts of new ventures over the next few months, and your commitment will be sorely tested. Although you may not at first be aware of it, the Light of the Old Ones will shine from your eyes, and their symbol will be all round you. Those who have walked the same paths will recognise you, and you may find new friends arriving or old acquaintances turning away because they feel this new power about you. Things in your life will change and for several months may be quite difficult as you adapt to the role you have freely accepted.

It does help to prepare well before you begin such an exercise. Choose a day in a waxing moon so that her power will help you, although you could use your own birthday or a special date in the year regardless of the phase of the moon. Put on clean clothes or better still, something kept just for magic, a robe, kaftan or special belt even. Take off your watch and put aside money, for that has no value at all in the Otherworld. It is your personal commitment which indicates wealth on the Hidden Road, and those things which are necessary to you will arrive in payment of the work you do.

This may not sound as exciting as an initiation ceremony into a coven, but I can assure you that those who have tried both will say this personal dedication takes a lot of beating as a magical event. Like much of the old lore it is simple, and it is unique, for you are creating the pattern of it just for yourself, just for the time of its performance. It cannot just be written in a book and repeated willy-nilly, as some people imagine magical work can be. Every single rite is an experiment and should be prepared as a one-off experience. The Old Ones do not seek sacrifices or offerings of things; they created them in the first place. We only borrow our bodies, our gardens and the things we use. They were once part of Nature and she will take them back in due time. We can only give of our own time and effort to bring about the changes in evolution that lead all of us towards the Light. This may be the first guttering candle you light, but in the end your soul may blaze like a star.

Exercises

If you have read any of the many books on modern witchcraft you will know all about actual initiation ceremonies, the oaths, and taking of a measure with a cord by the priestess, and all kinds of things of dramatic and impressive nature. On your own you will have only the Old Ones to contend with and they have no book so your experience will be individual and unique, if you are ready to follow the instructions for the dedication here. As you will have discovered, a lot of the material cannot just be written down and passed on like a cookery book. The recipes are given but you have to work out for yourself, with inner guidance, how to complete the process. If what you come up with seems untheatrical and simple, then it is probably far closer to the old way things were done than some of the elaborate and lengthy rites in modern books. Perhaps by now you will have had sufficient personal experiences to compensate for the inevitable disappointment about the down-to-earth nature of this old knowledge. What you have seen, heard, felt, 'imagined' even, cannot be shared by others, for they do not walk in your shoes nor dream your dreams.

Re-read all your notes and in the days leading up to your personal dedication be very sure you are happy and confident about the step you may soon be taking. There is no hurry. Some people have known about the Otherworld and the Hidden Ways for decades and not felt ready, and then suddenly known instinctively that it was time to proceed. Judge only by your own feelings, longings, intuitions and desires and you won't go wrong.

Begin your preparations slowly, meditating and even performing divinations to see if all is ready. Get your robe or other magical 'garment' ready, if you have chosen to make one. Think about your aims and the main direction you wish your work to follow in the coming years. Are you best at divination, at healing, at spells and talismans, or are you a poet or songsmith, or rescuer of lost knowledge? Each has a special task in the traditional crafts. Some are craftworkers, making beautiful or useful things, others create rituals, design worshipping prayers, or handle power. Some are seers or oracles, speaking with the voices of the Goddess, others are guides through the inner realms, relearning the narratives of inner journeys, telling tales, and refining knowledge with carefully chosen words.

You will have to study this chapter and gather the things you need, building up your own poems, gestures, food for the feast, flowers for the seasonal garland. You may also wish to make a witch's chaplet, a kind of rosary by which important things are remembered. Traditionally this is a length of ordinary rope, about four or five feet long. At one end there is a loop with the rope turned back on itself and spliced, and then there are eight equally spaced knots, equating to the planets and the Earth. The last knot is at the end of the rope so when it is tucked through the loop, a circle is made. Each knot and loop counts as one of the Nine Festivals. This can be used as a circle on the ground, with the staff outside, or tied to the staff at the centre of a space with a stick put through the loop to mark out a circle on the ground.

Think about your connection with the Goddess, and see if your dreams suggest the name you should take, or the animal, plant or flower or other natural thing which will be your passport to the Otherworld.

Planning and performing the dedication, along with regular inner journeys, meditations and keeping your Book up to date, will take up all of the twelfth moon.

Here are some more books to read:

Margot Adler, *Drawing Down the Moon* (Plymbridge Distributors)
Janet and Stewart Farrar, *The Witches' Goddess* and *The Witches' God* (Hale)
T C Lethbridge, *Witches* (Routledge and Kegan Paul)
R J Stewart, *The Underworld Initiation* (Aquarian)
Dion Fortune, *The Training and Work of an Initiate* (Aquarian)
Evan John Jones, *Witchcraft – An Old Tradition Revived* (Hale)

13.

COMPLETING THE CIRCLE

The witches have never acknowledged the limitations of the sense-world; they have always lived, moved and had their being in the domain where the subtle forces, now called Extra Sensory Perception, operate. The importance they place upon a linkage with this level of consciousness is expressed in the words of a present day witch: 'Once a person has had even one of these experiences of contacting forces beyond the world of form, he or she is no longer in bondage to it.'

Justine Glass: *Witchcraft: the Sixth Sense*

All the way through this book I have been trying to show the reader that there are ways every individual, given a bit of patience, common sense and determination, can awaken ancient sleeping powers from within themselves. Simply copying out 'rituals' from some earlier source, insisting that the festivals have to be celebrated on a particular calendar date (which is exactly what the early Christian Church did, to bring all its adherents into line) or insisting that a fixed structure of 'covens' with High Priestesses and High Priests is the only way witchcraft can be approached, is not satisfactory. Certainly there are many excellent covens with wonderful rituals, powerful Priests and Priestesses and fascinating sequences of seasonal sabbats, but it is not the only way. There are, of course, as in every other field of human existence, frauds and tricksters, people who claim a rare heritage of magic, initiations beyond anyone's belief, powers over all kinds of people or situations, and rip-off merchants ready to rook the unwary or untrained. One of the most important aspects of solo working is that you only have yourself to deal with, and your own fantasies or hang-ups to confront. Once you have actually made contact with the Old Ones you know that you are not alone and unsupported.

What saddens me is those people who have taken up witchcraft quite sincerely, practised its arts, celebrated full moons and festivals for years on the basis only of material taken from one or two books, or just the words of one hierarchy. Some of them have been too blinkered or even forbidden to use their own heads to think about the roots of the Craft, or the pattern of rituals. It is necessary to go beyond the written word, the published rites and seek the pure spring of ancient wisdom which in many forms has flowed throughout all lands, during our human childhood on this planet.

Learn something about the social structure before our modern times. Do you consider that large groups of people, many of whom would be members of large and extensive families, would be able to gather somewhere, waving swords and incense burners, dancing and chanting the names of the gods and goddesses of pagandom without some record of such events occurring somewhere? Don't you think that a pagan priesthood, which not only admitted priestesses but often held them in regard above the male priests, would have been recorded in some document somewhere in Europe in the last thousand years or so? Even the witch trials, which suggested all sorts of impossible things, never caught on to the idea of female priests! Look at the fuss that is being made these days about the ordination of women into the Church of England – when you could be hanged for unnatural practices, don't you suppose that some bright inquisitor might have thought of accusing ladies of being pagan priestesses and worshipping a Goddess? Flying through the air on hurdles was quite reasonable and sexual congress with goats all par for the course, but preserving ancient gods and goddesses, dancing at high, sacred sites, casting magical circles and gathering in covens led by a priestess fortunately never seem to have crossed their bigoted minds. Surely this suggests that they never happened!

We do know that magic has existed since the days of the cave-dwellers. Their elaborate paintings and carvings demonstrate this, and recent research is adding to our understanding of the symbolism of ancient art all the time. We know that it still works, or the tens of thousands of witches, magicians, 'wiccans', occultists, Qabalists and shamans would not make any effort to study and practise a useless art. Today psychology is exploring the minds of people, finding there the impulses which can lead to physical illness, or the inner strengths by which healing power from within can overcome cancers or arthritis. They are teaching relaxation methods which lower blood pressure and the levels of stress chemicals in the system. They are using 'creative visualisation' to enhance concentration in both children and older folk. They are using very nearly purely magical methods of storytelling and confidence-building techniques to return to individuals those inherent powers which they feel they have lost or never had.

It is in the works of Jung and his followers that we find credence given to the validity of symbolism and mythology; an acceptance that alchemy was not just an early attempt at organic chemistry, but a way of discovering the mental transformations a person could make towards individual evolution, purifying their purpose and motives. The need to break themselves down, as it were, into chemical elements, to be burned, whitened, changed and recombined are very similar concepts to those which Russian shamans went through, being torn apart by wild animals and reborn healed and renewed.

Within the books written by modern ceremonial magicians the lone witch will also find much valuable information and insight, for ritualists have often worked alone, from the days of Merlin to this century. They do band together into structured Lodges for certain aspects of the work, but most of them learn the arts of meditation and the crafts and skills of talisman making and divination and use these as solo workers. Although the ceremonial magicians of today have a very complicated system of setting up rituals, invoking the powers of angels and building the inner images of temples and places of power, their actual work is much more suited to the individual practitioner because all along, stress is laid upon the mental aspects, which are often ignored in books on witchcraft. The idea of blessing the four Quarters in the names of the archangels can easily be replaced with the use of the Elements themselves, and the description of the indoor room of an ancient temple exchanged for the greenwood setting of the Great Goddess and her Companion.

Much of the real work of magic has to be done on the inner levels in any case, no matter who is involved, where it physically takes place or what system is being used. Once you know how to switch your awareness into the 'searching for wisdom mode' you can flick through library books, subconsciously settling upon a valid quote or relevant piece of

information. This is how the old witches used to work. In their
ordinary lives they would have encountered many bits of data,
just as we do, but when an animal was sick they would be able
to sift through the hedge and find a suitable herb, depending on
the season, or cast their mind back to the last charm against fire
in the thatch for a client seeking that sort of protection.
(Incidentally, the zigzag-shaped iron end-plates on supporting
struts seen on cottage walls are the rune Sigel, the Sun, which is
intended to prevent lightning strikes, and the Xs are the rune
Geoffu, the Giver, thought to bring luck.)

Gradually you will find that your intuition wakes up, that
you regularly have hunches. You should learn to act on these
and not spend time trying to rationalise what is coming directly
to you by divine inspiration. Act immediately and you will put
up your success rate by 95%. It is hard in a logical world to rely
on this unexpected source of common wisdom, but once you get
it going life's little problems fall away. You find that you can
buy bargains in old junk shops to suit your unlikely need, or
find a parking space in a crowded city centre, simply by pausing
on your journey and 'listening' for that inner voice of guidance.

Knowledge will start to flow to you from unlikely sources.
Strangers will approach you with important pieces of
information, books will fall off shelves at your feet or spring
open at just the page you need. Snippets of radio or TV
programmes will offer a crumb of knowledge just when you
were wondering how on earth you could locate that address, or
book title or whatever. You may discover other members of
your family have records or memories of long-forgotten facts
about your grandparents which open up whole fields of further
research, or that old tools or photographs turn up in the loft and
point you off in another direction in your search for blood links
with pagan ideas.

You stop losing things very quickly because you have a sense
of attachment to things that have a habit of wandering. If they
do disappear you will find a sharp command 'Bring my keys
back *now*' will often have the desired effect and they will
materialise under the hall table. You will be guided to write to
people, or telephone just at the moment when something you
wanted to know comes to light. You will find ways of protecting
your house and property from thieves or vandals, and your
garden from blight, if you ask the Great Guardian God to take a
hand, or the Lady of growing things to protect your roses.

These things are trivial; they require much more in the way of trust of the improbable than book learning or coven training. They cannot really be written down because the vast majority of material of value to modern solo witches has to be experienced, tried and tested and found good. You will have to continue to experiment, reaching out all the time to understand without intellectually analysing or logically dissecting what you have to do. Keep your brain from interfering with what your heart knows best how to deal with; allow images and ideas to flow like a river, not be caught in bucketfuls by the inquisitive mind, which always has 'How does it work?' on its tongue.

Magic and all the old arts work because the Goddess who is mother to our world wishes it, and because the Great Cosmic Father is amused by our little workings, and shares the joy of our festivals. Once we are able to enter that free-thinking realm then we will be truly free, and our magic will both guide us and satisfy us with its positive results. We have a right to be as wise as our ancestors, and to inherit their traditional abilities to work in harmony with Nature for the good of Nature, and for all living beings, of whom we are a small example.

Our magical circle is the great ring of the circling stars. They are our kindred and sources of our mundane power, if we learn that Light is not just illumination to see by but a path to follow, and a lantern which each of us in turn may take up and so guide the footsteps of others wandering in the lonely dark. We have to begin to think globally, so that our magic skills will benefit those all round this beautiful green Earth, and that the spiritual example we are able to set by our lives can inspire and support many others.

You can learn to be a witch, a Wise Woman, a Cunning Man, a healer, a diviner, a magician, a pagan or any other thing you will, on your own, but you will never be lonely for there are thousands out there, on the same path. Some are ahead of you, some behind, some lost and unsure and perhaps scared because they do not have your confidence, gained from your experiences and training no matter how unfinished, and you will be able to offer help, albeit mentally or spiritually.

The exercises which complete the year are up to you. Seek out true companions on the inner ways, make contact with the Goddess and the God as you are coming to know them. Meditate or look inwards at your own growing spark of divine light, and be prepared to shine before those of the Earth who are lost in material matters. Set out your sacred place, on a world which is sacred all over yet often spoiled by the acts of humanity. Learn and practise your divining arts, your practical crafts, your magics and your healing powers. Give thanks always to the Great Ones, walk gently in their ways, honour their symbols and look for their Light which shines from the eyes of those who know them wherever you go.

May they bless your life.

Marian Green would be happy to receive letters from anyone who is trying out the exercises in this book and will reply, time permitting, if return postage or International Reply Coupons are enclosed.

Marian Green is the Editor of QUEST magazine, published since 1970, and available only from BCM-SCL QUEST, London WC1N 3XX, UK. She also runs one- and two-day courses in Britain, Europe and Canada; details from QUEST.

Here are just a few more books!

R J Stewart, *Advanced Magical Arts* (Element Books)
Will Parfitt, *The Living Qabalah* (Element Books)
W E Butler, *Apprenticed to Magic* (Aquarian)
Dion Fortune, *The Cosmic Doctrine* (Aquarian)
Rae Beth, *Hedge Witch* (Hale)
Janet and Stewart Farrar, *Spells and How They Work* (Hale)
Margaret Murray, *The Witchcult in Western Europe* (Oxford University Press)
Monica Sjoo, *The Great Cosmic Mother of All* (Rainbow Press, Trondheim)
Basil Wilby, *A History of White Magic* (Mowbrays)
Paddy Slade, *Natural Magic* (Hamlyn)

INDEX